THE SCIENCE

of

GETTING RICH

⚜

THE SCIENCE
of
GETTING RICH

———— ⚜ ————

Wallace D. Wattles

Edited by Ruth L. Miller

ATRIA BOOKS
New York London Toronto Sydney

ATRIA BOOKS
A Division of Simon & Schuster, Inc.
1230 Avenue of the Americas
New York, NY 10020

BEYOND WORDS PUBLISHING
20827 N.W. Cornell Road, Suite 500
Hillsboro, Oregon 97124–9808
503-531-8700 tel
503-531-8773 fax
www.beyondword.com

Managing editors: Henry Covi, Lindsay S. Brown
Copyediting/proofreading: Gretchen Stelter, Kayla Ballrot
Design/composition: Nancy Singer Olaguera, ISPN Publishing, Sara E. Blum

First Atria Books/Beyond Words hardcover edition September 2007

ATRIA BOOKS and colophon are trademarks of Simon & Schuster, Inc. Beyond Words Publishing is a division of Simon & Schuster, Inc.

For more information about special discounts for bulk purchases, please contact Simon & Schuster Special Sales at 1-800-456-6798 or business@simonandschuster.com

Manufactured in the United States of America

10 9 8 7 6 5 4 3 2 1

Library of Congress Control Number: 2007920783

ISBN-13: 978–1–58270–188–2
ISBN-10: 1–58270–188–1

The corporate mission of Beyond Words Publishing, Inc.: *Inspire to Integrity*

Dedicated to You

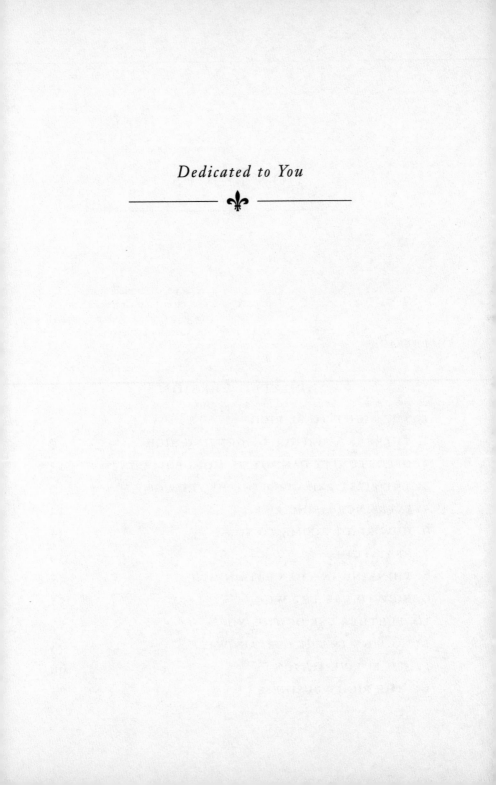

CONTENTS

❧

ORIGINAL TEXT

PREFACE

❧

THIS BOOK is pragmatic, not philosophic; a practical manual, not a treatise upon theories. It is intended for the men and women whose most pressing need is for money, who wish to get rich first and philosophize afterward. It is for those who have, so far, found neither the time, the means, nor the opportunity to go deeply into the study of metaphysics, but who want results and who are willing to take the conclusions of science as a basis for action, without going into all the processes by which those conclusions were reached.

It is expected that the reader will take the fundamental statements upon faith, just as he would take statements concerning a law of electrical action if they were promulgated by a Marconi or an Edison; and, taking the statements upon faith, that he will prove their truth by acting upon them without fear or hesitation. Every man or woman who does this will certainly get rich; for the science applied herein is an exact science, and failure is impossible. For the benefit, however, of those who wish to investigate philosophical theories and so secure a logical basis for faith, I will here cite certain authorities.

The monistic theory of the universe, the theory that One is All and that All is One; that one Substance manifests itself as the seeming many elements of the material world, is of Hindu origin and has been gradually winning its way into the thought of the western world for two hundred years. It is the foundation of all the Oriental philosophies and of those of Descartes, Spinoza, Leibnitz, Schopenhauer, Hegel, and Emerson.

The reader who would dig to the philosophical foundations of this is advised to read Hegel and Emerson.

In writing this book, I have sacrificed all other considerations to plainness and simplicity of style, so that all might understand. The plan of action laid down herein was deduced from the conclusions of philosophy; it has been thoroughly tested and bears the supreme test of practical experiment: it works. If you wish to know how the conclusions were arrived at, read the writings of the authors mentioned above; and if you wish to reap the fruits of their philosophies in actual practice, read this book and do exactly as it tells you to do.

—*W. D. Wattles*

UPDATED VERSION

1. THE RIGHT TO BE RICH

---------- ⚜ ----------

WHATEVER MAY be said in praise of poverty, the fact remains that no one can live a really complete or successful life unless they're rich. We can't achieve our greatest potential unless we have plenty of money; for to develop our gifts and talents, we must use many things, and we can't have those things unless we have money to buy them with.

People develop themselves—mind, soul, and body—by using things and going places, and in today's money oriented society, we must spend money to have those things and go those places. Our world has advanced so far and become so complex that even the most ordinary man or woman requires a great amount of wealth, compared to any time in the past, to come even close to fulfillment.

An Inalienable Right

All of life has one purpose: development. Everyone naturally wants to become all that they are capable of becoming. It's inherent in human nature; we can't help wanting to be all that we can be! And everything that lives has an inalienable right to all the development it's capable of attaining (our Founding Fathers called this "the pursuit of happiness"). Everyone has the right to the free and unrestricted use of all the things they need for their fullest mental, spiritual, and physical development. In short, we all have the right to be rich.

In this book, I'm not talking figuratively or just about psychological or emotional riches. To be really rich does *not* mean to be satisfied or contented with a little. No one should be satisfied with a little if they're capable of using and enjoying more. Nature's purpose is to advance and develop all of life, which means that everyone should have all that can contribute to the power, elegance, beauty, and richness of their life, and to be content with less is contrary to nature's intent.

The Desire for a Richer Life

There's nothing wrong with wanting to get rich. A desire for riches is really the desire for a richer, fuller, and more abundant life, and that desire is praiseworthy. Anyone who owns all they want to live all the life they're capable of living is rich, and, in our world, no one who hasn't got plenty of money can have all they want. Anyone who doesn't want enough money to buy all that they desire is denying their true nature.

Success in life is becoming what you want to be. You can become all you want to be only by making use of things, and you can have the free use of things only as you become rich enough to acquire them. So, understanding the science of getting rich is the most essential of all knowledge.

Living Fully

Three aspects of our being need to be developed: the body, the mind, and the soul. No one of these is better or holier than the other; they're all equally desirable, and no one of the three—body, mind, or soul—can live fully if either of the others is deprived of full life and expression. It's neither right nor noble to live only for the soul and deny mind or body, and it's wrong to live for the intellect and deny the body or soul.

We've all seen the painful consequences of living for the body and denying both mind and soul, and we see that to live a full life means the complete expression of all three. Whatever they might say, no one can be really happy or satisfied unless their body is living fully in every function and unless the same is true of their mind and their soul, as well.

Wherever there's a possibility unexpressed or one of these functions unperformed, we experience unsatisfied desire. Desire can be defined, therefore, as "possibility seeking expression or function seeking performance."

No one can live fully in body without good food, comfortable clothing, and warm shelter, and without freedom from excessive toil. Periodic rest and recreation are also needed.

No one can live fully in mind without books or media and time to study them, without opportunities for travel and observation, or without intellectual companionship. In fact, to live fully in mind, we must have interests to explore and must surround ourselves with all the objects of art and beauty we're capable of using and appreciating.

To live fully in soul, we must have love, and love can't be fully expressed when we're stuck in poverty. This is because love finds its most natural and spontaneous expression in giving: our highest happiness is found in providing the blessings of life to those we love. People who have nothing to give can't really fill their role as a spouse or parent, as a citizen, or as a human being.

Clearly, it's in the use of material things that anyone finds full life for the body, develops the mind, and unfolds the soul. It's therefore supremely important for us to be rich.

Fulfilling Our Duty

It's perfectly right that you should desire to be rich. If you're a normal man or woman, you can't help doing so. It's perfectly right that you give your best attention to the science of getting rich, for it's the most fundamental of all studies.

In fact, to neglect this study is to be derelict in your duty to yourself, to God, and to humanity, for the highest service you can render to God and humanity is to make the most of yourself.

SUMMARY

No one can achieve their greatest potential unless they have plenty of money, for to develop our gifts and talents, we must use many things and go many places, and unless we have money, we can't.

A desire for riches is really the desire for a richer, fuller, and more abundant life, and that desire is praiseworthy.

No one can be really happy or satisfied unless their body is living fully in every way, and the same is true of their mind and their soul, as well.

It's perfectly right that you should give your best attention to the science of getting rich because it's fundamental to all studies, and the highest service you can render to God and humanity is to make the most of yourself.

2. THERE IS A SCIENCE OF GETTING RICH

———————— ⚜ ————————

THERE'S A science of getting rich, and it's an exact science, like chemistry or arithmetic. Certain laws govern the process, and once anyone learns and obeys these laws, they will get rich. No doubt about it. Acquiring money and property comes from doing things in a certain way, and those who do things this certain way, whether on purpose or accidentally, get rich, while those who don't do things this way, no matter how hard they work or how able they are, remain poor.

The science is based on the natural law that states: *like causes always produce like effects.*[1] This law works in the same way as the law of gravity or any other natural law: it applies equally to everyone, everywhere. Everyone has the choice to act in accordance with it or to ignore it, but we all experience its consequences. So anyone who learns to create the causes that produce riches will automatically get rich. Anyone.

---

1 Christians teach this principle as "you reap what you sow."

It's Not the Environment

It can happen anywhere. Getting rich isn't a matter of environment; if it were, all the people in certain neighborhoods would become wealthy. The people of one city would all be rich, while those of other towns would all be poor, or everyone who lived in one state would roll in wealth, while those of an adjoining state would be stuck in poverty. But everywhere we see rich and poor living side-by-side, in the same environment, and often doing the same kinds of work.

When two people are in the same business in the same vicinity and one gets rich while the other remains poor, it shows us that getting rich is not primarily a matter of environment. Some environments may be more favorable than others, but when two people in the same business are in the same neighborhood and one gets rich while the other fails, it indicates that getting rich is the result of some other factor.

It's Not About Talent

Nor is getting rich due to how talented one is, for many people who have great talent remain poor, while others who have very little talent get rich. In fact, studying people who have gotten rich shows that they're pretty average, with no greater talents and abilities than most other people have. They don't get rich because of any special talent they might have but because they happen to do things in the certain way that produces riches.

It's Not About Thrift

Getting rich is not the result of being careful how you spend money. Many thrifty people are poor, while free spenders often get rich. Nor is getting rich due to doing business differently than others, for often two people in the same business do almost exactly the same things and one gets rich while the other remains poor or even goes bankrupt.

It's clear then that getting rich is simply the result of doing things in a certain way. And if anyone who does things that way becomes rich, then what we're talking about is a science.

It's Not Difficult

The question then becomes whether this science is too difficult for most people to do. Well, if we look around us, we can see the answer: talented people get rich and blockheads get rich; intellectually brilliant people get rich and very stupid people get rich; physically strong people get rich and weak or sickly people get rich. Some degree of ability to think and understand is, of course, essential, but all the evidence says that anyone who has sense enough to read and understand these words can certainly get rich.

It's Not What Business You're In

Again, it's not a matter of any particular business or profession. People get rich in every business and in every profession, while their next-door neighbors, in the very same line of work, might remain in poverty.

It is true that you'll do best in a business that you like and is congenial to you. And if you have certain talents that are well developed, you'll do best in a business that uses those talents. Also, you'll do best in a business that's suited to your locality: an ice cream parlor would do better in a warm climate than in Greenland, and a salmon fishery will succeed better in the Pacific Northwest than in Florida, where there are no salmon.

But, aside from these general limitations, your getting rich doesn't depend on any particular business you might go into;

it only depends on your learning to do things in a certain way. If you're now in business and anybody else in your locality is getting rich in the same business while you aren't, it's simply because you're not doing things in the same way they are.

It's Not Your Location

Yes, location counts for something. No one would go to the heart of Antarctica or the Sahara and expect to run a successful business! Getting rich involves dealing with people and being where there are people to deal with, and if these people are inclined to deal in the way you want to deal, so much the better. But that's it as far as environment goes. If anybody else in your town can get rich, so can you, and if anybody else in your state can get rich, so can you.

It Doesn't Require Capital

No one is prevented from getting rich by lack of funds or capital. True, as you build capital, it increases more easily and rapidly, but anyone who has capital is already rich and doesn't need to learn how to become so. No matter how poor you may be, if you begin to do things according to this science, you will begin to get rich and you will begin to build capital. The building of capital is part of the process of getting rich, and it is part of the result that invariably follows doing things in the certain way described by this science.

It's About Obeying Universal Laws

You may be the poorest person on the continent and deeply in debt. You may not have friends, influence, or resources, but if you begin to do things this way, you must inevitably begin to get rich, for like causes *must* produce like effects. If you have no capital, you can get capital. If you're in the wrong business, you can get into the right business. If you're in the wrong location, you can go to the right location.

And you can do so by beginning in your present business and in your present location to do things the certain way that always causes success. You simply must begin to live in harmony with the laws that govern the universe.

SUMMARY

The science of getting rich is based on the natural law that like causes always produce like effects. Anyone who learns to create the causes that produce riches will automatically get rich.

It's not the environment; everywhere we see rich and poor living side-by-side and often doing the same kinds of work.

It's not about talent; many people who have great talent remain poor, while others who have very little talent get rich.

It's not about being thrifty; many thrifty people are poor, while free spenders often get rich.

It's not difficult. Some degree of ability to think and understand is, of course, essential, but anyone who has sense enough to read and understand these words can certainly get rich.

It's not what business you're in. People get rich in every business and in every profession, though you'll do best in a business that you like and is congenial to you. Also, you'll do best in a business that's suited to your locality, but your getting rich doesn't depend on any particular business you might go into.

It's not your location; if anybody else in your town can get rich, so can you, and if anybody else in your state can get rich, so can you.

It doesn't require capital. No matter how poor you may be, if you begin to do things according to this science, you will begin to get rich and you will begin to build capital.

3. OPPORTUNITY CANNOT BE MONOPOLIZED

———— ⚜ ————

No ONE is poor because someone else monopolized the world's wealth and put a fence around it. Businesses and bosses do not hold people back. For the most part, people who work for others—whether as laborers, clerks, managers, or professionals—are where they are because they don't do things in the certain way that makes them rich.

The law of riches is the same for them as it is for all others, so members of the "working class" may become the "upper class" whenever they begin to do things this certain way. Until they learn this, they'll remain where they are, struggling to make ends meet and subject to the whims of the economy.

Others' ignorance of the law does not hold anyone down. Anyone can follow the tide of opportunity to riches, and this book will tell them how.

There's No Limit to Supply
You can't be deprived of opportunity. There may be times when you're prevented from certain lines of business, but

there are always other channels open to you. The tide of opportunity moves in different directions, according to the needs of the whole and the state of the society, and those who go with the tide, instead of trying to swim against it, find an abundance of opportunities.

No one is kept in poverty by limits in the supply of riches; there's more than enough for all. A palace as large as the capitol building in Washington could be built for every family on earth from the building material in the U. S. alone, and under intensive cultivation, this country would produce wool, cotton, linen, and silk enough to clothe everybody in the world beautifully, together with food enough to feed them all luxuriously.

In truth, the visible supply is practically inexhaustible, and the invisible supply really is inexhaustible.

This is because everything we see on earth is made from one original substance, out of which all things proceed. New forms are constantly being made and older ones are dissolving, but all are made out of one thing.

And there's no limit to this formless substance. The universe is made out of it, but it was not all used in making the universe. The spaces in, through, and between the forms of the visible universe are permeated and filled with this original substance, the raw material of all things. Ten thousand times as much as has been made might still be made, and we still would not have exhausted the supply of universal raw material.

Nature is an unlimited storehouse of riches; the supply will never run short.

Infinite Substance Always Meets Humanity's Needs
Original substance is alive with creative energy and is constantly producing more forms. When the current

supply of building material is exhausted, a new kind will be produced. If the soil is exhausted so that foods and materials for clothing will no longer grow, it will be renewed or more soil will be made. When all the gold and silver has been dug from the earth, if humanity still needs gold and silver, more will be produced from the formless. The formless stuff responds to the needs of mankind; it will not let humanity be without any good thing.

The formless substance is alive and is always impelled toward more life. It is conscious intelligence: it's stuff that thinks. And the natural and inherent impulse of life is to seek to live more; the nature of intelligence is to expand, and consciousness always seeks new frontiers and finds fuller expression.

The universe is a great living presence, always moving toward more life and fuller functioning. Nature exists for the advancement of life, and its primary impulse is the increase of life. Because of this, everything that can possibly enhance life is bountifully provided.

Humanity, therefore, is always abundantly rich, and if individuals are poor, it's because they don't follow the certain way of doing things that makes someone rich.

No one is poor because nature is poor or because there's not enough to go around. You are not kept poor by a lack in the supply of riches. I'll demonstrate later that even the resources of the formless supply are at the command of whoever will act and think in a certain way.

SUMMARY

Nobody is held back by others.

You can't be deprived of opportunity. Those who go with the tide, instead of trying to swim against it, find an abundance of opportunity.

No one is kept in poverty by limits in the supply of riches; there's more than enough for all. Everything we see on earth is made from one original substance, out of which all things proceed, and there's no limit to this formless substance.

Nature is formed for the advancement of life, and its primary impulse is the increase of life. Because of this, everything that can possibly enhance life is bountifully provided.

4. THE FIRST PRINCIPLE
IN THE SCIENCE

———— ⚜ ————

THOUGHT IS the only power that can produce tangible riches from the formless substance. In fact, original substance only moves according to thoughts: the thought of a particular form in substance produces that form. This means that every form and process you see in nature is the visible expression of a thought in original substance.[2] As the formless stuff thinks of a form, it takes that form; as it thinks of a motion, it makes that motion. This is how all things were created.

Substance Takes and Holds the Form of Thought
Thinking substance takes the form of its thought, moves according to the thought, and maintains itself in the form of that thought.

We live in a thought world, which is part of a thought universe. The thought of a moving universe extended throughout

———————

2 In quantum physics, these principles are stated as, "matter exists only in the presence of an observer; everything takes form out of the quantum field, or substrate, as a result of perception."

formless substance, then the thinking stuff moved according to that thought to take the form of systems of stars and planets, and now it maintains that form.

Though it may take centuries to do the work, the substance, holding the idea of a circling system of suns and worlds, takes the form of these bodies and moves them as it thinks. Thinking the form of a slow growing oak tree, it moves accordingly and produces the tree.

In creating, the formless seems to move according to already established lines of motion. In other words, the thought of an oak tree doesn't cause a full-grown tree to take form instantly but starts in motion the processes that will produce the tree along established lines of growth.

Every thought of form, held in thinking substance, causes the creation of that form, but the creative process tends to move along lines of growth and action already established. In another example, as the thought of a specific style of house is impressed upon formless substance, it might not cause the house to instantly appear, but it would cause creative energies already working in the economy and community to result in the rapid building of the house.

And if there were no existing channels through which the creative energy could work, then the house would be formed directly from primal substance, without waiting for the slow processes of the organic and inorganic world to unfold.

Human Thoughts Take Form in Substance

No thought of form can be impressed upon original substance without causing the creation of the form. All human beings originate thought, and all the forms anybody fashions with the hands first exist in thought. We cannot make a thing until we have thought that thing.

So far, humanity has confined its efforts to seeking to change or modify what already exists. Nearly everyone merely reshapes and modifies existing forms by manual labor or machines. When people think of a form, they take material from already existing forms in nature and modify that material to make an image of the form that is in their mind.

Most of us don't even consider whether we could produce things from the formless substance directly, by communicating our thoughts into it. We've not dreamed that we can do what we see the Creator doing.

I propose to prove that we can and to show how.

We start with three fundamental statements:

There is one original formless stuff or substance from which all things are made.

All the seemingly many elements are but different variations of the one element.

All the many organic and inorganic forms found in nature are just different shapes of the same stuff; thoughts held in the substance produce the form of the thought.

Clearly, if someone can communicate a thought to this original intelligent substance, he can cause the creation, or formation, of the thing he or she thinks about.

It may be asked if I can prove these statements and, without going into details, I answer that I can do so, both by logic and experience.

From my observations of form and thought, I reason back to one original thinking substance. And reasoning forward from this thinking substance, I come to a person's power to cause the formation of the thing he thinks about, as in the preceding paragraphs.

Then, by experiment, the reasoning proves true. This is my strongest proof. If one person who reads this book gets rich by doing what it says to do, that is evidence supporting my claim, but if *everyone* who does what it says gets rich, that is positive proof, until someone goes through the process and fails. The theory is true until the process fails, and this process will not fail, *for everyone who does exactly what this book says to do gets rich.*

Learning What to Think is the Key

I've said that people get rich by doing things in a certain way, and, in order to do things that way, people must learn to think a certain way.

The way we do things is the direct result of the way we think about things. So to do things the way you want to do them, you have to learn to think the way you want to think. And to think what you really *want* to think is to think Truth, regardless of appearances. This is the first step toward getting rich.

Everyone is born with the power to think what he or she wants to think, but it takes far more effort to do so than it does to think the thoughts suggested by what we see or hear. To think according to the appearances of our senses is easy; to think Truth regardless of appearances takes effort—and more energy than any other work we will ever do.

There's no effort people will avoid as much as they avoid sustained and consistent thought. It's the hardest work in the world. This is especially true when the thought they wish to sustain is contrary to appearances.

But every appearance in the visible world tends to produce a corresponding form in the mind that observes it, and this can only be prevented by holding the thought of the Truth, regardless of the appearance.

Observing the appearances of poverty produces corresponding forms in your own mind, unless you hold to the truth that there is no poverty, only abundance. To think health when surrounded by the appearances of disease or to think riches when in the midst of the appearances of poverty requires effort, but whoever develops this power becomes a Mastermind. These are the people who can conquer fate and have what they want.

We can only develop this power by realizing the basic fact behind all appearances: there is one intelligent substance all things are made of and by. Then we must grasp the truth that every thought held in this substance becomes a form, and that someone can so impress his thoughts upon it as to cause them to take form and become visible things. When we realize this, we lose all doubt and fear, for we know that we can create what we want to create, we can get what we want to have, and we can become what we want to be.

Making It a Habit is Essential

You must lay aside all other concepts of the universe, and you must contemplate this idea until it's fixed in your mind as your habitual thought. Read these statements over and over again. Fix every word in your memory and meditate on them until you firmly believe what they say. If a doubt comes to you, cast it aside. Don't listen to arguments against this idea.

Don't go to churches or lectures where contrary ideas are taught or preached. Don't read magazines or books that teach a different idea. If you get mixed up in your understanding, belief, or faith, all your efforts will be in vain.

Don't ask why these things are true or speculate as to how they can be true. For the time being, simply take them on trust. The science of getting rich begins with the absolute acceptance of this fundamental idea.

SUMMARY

There is an intelligent substance from which all things are made and which, in its original state, permeates, penetrates, and fills all the interspaces of the universe.

Any thought in this substance produces the thing that is imaged by the thought.

All the forms that anyone fashions with his hands must first exist in his thought. We cannot shape a thing until we have thought that thing.

Anyone can form things in thought and, by impressing that thought upon formless substance, can cause the thing to be created.

The key is holding the desired thought, the Truth, in spite of all appearances.

5 . EVER-INCREASING LIFE

⎯⎯⎯⎯⎯ ⚜ ⎯⎯⎯⎯⎯

IT'S TIME to let go of any last remains of the idea that it's any deity's will that you be poor or that you serve anyone by remaining in poverty.[3] The divine, whether called God, our Father, Christ, Brahman, Great Spirit, the Goddess, or the Tao, is the fundamental principle of the universe, represented by the essential qualities of Life, Intelligence, Wisdom, and Love. To understand the workings of these qualities is, therefore, to see God at work and to understand God's will for all of us.

A seed dropped into the ground springs into activity, and simply in the act of living, produces a hundred more seeds. So Life, simply by living, multiplies itself. It's forever becoming more. It *must* do so in order to continue being.

Intelligence has this same need to constantly increase; consciousness is continually expanding. Every thought we

⎯⎯⎯⎯⎯

3 Note that the writer is not saying that God doesn't exist—merely that too many of us believe that the ultimate divinity wants us to suffer or be poor. Nowhere in the Bible, Torah, Koran, or Vedas does it say that riches are evil or that being wealthy is a bad thing. Jesus is described as saying, "The love of money is the root of all evil," which in no way contradicts what's being said

think inspires us to think another thought. Knowledge is continually increasing; every fact we learn leads us to another fact. Every talent we develop awakens the desire to develop another talent. We're all subject to the urge of Life seeking expression, driving us on to know more, to do more, and to be more.

The intelligent substance that is all in all, that lives in all and lives in you, is a conscious, living substance. Being a consciously living substance, it must have the same nature and inherent desire to increase Life that is in every living intelligence. Every living thing must continually seek to enlarge its life because Life, in the mere act of living, must increase itself.

In order to know more, do more, and be more we must have more and have access to even more than we have ourselves. *We must get rich so we can live more fully*.

So get rid of the idea that God wants you to sacrifice yourself for others and that you can secure heavenly favor by doing so. God requires nothing of the kind. What God wants is for you to make the most of yourself, for yourself and for others. And you can help others more by making the most of yourself than in any other way.

Nature, Desiring the Fulfillment of our Desires

The desire for riches is simply our own capacity for larger life seeking fulfillment. What makes you want more money—and the resources that come with it—is what makes the

---

here; resources are to be acquired for what they can help us do and be—not for their own sake. Jesus is also quoted as saying, "blessed are the poor in spirit..." To be "poor in spirit" is not to be without funds or resources, but to avoid "lording it over" others; to have the humility to recognize that no one is better than anyone else, and to recognize that it is "not I, but the Father within who does the work."

plant grow: Life seeking fuller expression. Every desire is an unexpressed possibility seeking to come into being, power seeking to manifest.

The one living substance out of which all things are made is subject to this inherent law of all life. It's permeated with the desire to live more fully, and that's why it must constantly create things. So the one substance is filled with desire to live more in and through you, and it wants you to have all the things you can use to do so.

The one substance in the universe is the one intelligence, which is God. Therefore *it's God's desire that you be rich*. God wants you to get rich because divinity can express itself more fully through you if you have plenty to use for expression. God, as the Father, the Christ, or the Buddha Nature, can live most fully in you if you have unlimited command of the means of life.

As we said before, the purpose of nature is the expansion of Life, so nature is friendly to your plans for fulfillment. Everything is naturally on your side. The universe desires you to have everything you want to have.

Make up your mind that this is true.

Harmony, Essential for Fulfillment

One limitation: *it's essential that your purpose be in harmony with the purpose that is in all*. This means you must want real Life, not mere pleasure or sensual gratification. And human beings really live only when we perform every function—physical, mental, and spiritual—of which we are capable, without excess in any.

You don't want to get rich just to gratify animal desires. That's not Life. But the performance of every physical function is a part of life, and no one lives completely who denies the impulses of the body their normal and healthful expression.

You don't want to get rich solely to enjoy mental pleasures, to gain knowledge, to gratify ambition, to outshine
others, to be famous. All these are a legitimate part of life,
but whoever lives for the pleasures of the intellect alone will
only have a partial life and will never be satisfied.

You don't want to get rich solely for the good of others,
to lose yourself in "saving the world," only experiencing the
joys of philanthropy and sacrifice. Remember that extreme
altruism is no better and no nobler than extreme selfishness; both are mistakes. All the great spiritual teachers have
shown us this. The joys of the soul are only a part of life, and
they're no better or nobler than any other part.

You want to get rich so you can eat, drink, and be merry
when it is time to do these things, so you can surround yourself with beautiful things, see distant lands, feed your mind,
and develop your intellect. You want to be able to love others and do kind things and, ultimately, to be able to do your
part in helping the world find fulfillment.

Competition and Sacrifice: Unnecessary and Useless

Remember, though, that substance is forming for all, and its
movements are always for more life to all. It can't be made
to work for less life to anyone because it seeks fulfillment
and wellbeing equally in all.

So, since intelligent substance will make things for you
but it won't take things away from someone else and give
them to you, you must rid yourself of the thought of competition. You are "made in the image of the Creator," here
to create, not to compete for what is already created.

You don't have to take anything away from anyone.

You don't have to drive sharp bargains.

You don't have to cheat or to take advantage, nor do you need to let anyone work for you for less than they deserve.

You don't have to covet the property of others or even look at it with wishful eyes. No one has anything so wonderful that you can't have the same or better—without taking what he has away from him. Riches secured through competition are never satisfactory and permanent; they're yours today and another's tomorrow.

You're going to get what you want, but in such a way that, when you get it, everyone you affect will have more than they have now. You become a creator, not a competitor, using your uniquely human faculties of perception, reason, will, memory, imagination, and intuition to form the substance around you into the object of your desire, enriching everyone around you in the process.

I'm aware that there are those who get a vast amount of money by acting in ways that contradict these statements so will add a word of explanation here. People who become very rich purely through competition sometimes unconsciously connect with substance in its great movements for the general improvement of society through economic development. The "robber barons" (Rockefeller, Carnegie, Morgan, et al.) of the 1890s through the 1920s were unconscious agents in the necessary work of organizing industry, and their work has contributed immensely toward increased life for all. But their day is over. They organized industrial production and were succeeded by those who organized distribution systems. Like the dinosaurs, they played a necessary part in the evolutionary process, but the same power that produced them disposed of them. And it's well to bear in mind that they were never really rich; records of their private lives show that they were usually pretty wretched.

Likewise, the greedy fund managers and CEOs of the 1980s and 1990s may have acquired millions, but they have suffered for it and, in the process, were the agents of global corporate and securities reform.

Remember, if you're to become rich using the methods of this science, *you must rise entirely out of competitive thought.* You must never think for a moment that the supply is limited. Just as soon as you begin to think all the money is being cornered and controlled by others and you must exert yourself to get laws passed to stop this process—in that moment, you drop from the creative mind into the competitive mind, and your power to create is gone for the time being.

And what's worse, you probably would have shut down the creative movements already beginning to work for you.

Thought Focused on Truth Formulates Desires
Never look at the visible supply. Instead, always look at the limitless riches in formless substance and *know* that they are coming to you as fast as you can receive and use them.

Know that there are countless millions of dollars' worth of gold in the mountains of the earth not yet brought to light. And know that if there were not, more would be created from thinking substance to supply your needs.

Know that the money you need is coming, even if it's necessary for a thousand men to be led to the discovery of new gold mines tomorrow.

Nobody, by cornering the visible supply, can prevent you from getting what is truly yours. So never allow yourself to think for an instant that all the best building sites will be taken before you're ready to build your house. Never worry about governments, trusts, or corporations, or fear they will soon come to own the whole earth. Never become afraid that you'll lose what you want because some other person beats you to it. That can't possibly happen!

You're not seeking anything that anyone else has; instead, you're causing what you want to be created from formless substance, and that supply is limitless. Stick to the principles of this science:

All things are made from a thinking stuff that, in its original state, permeates, penetrates, and fills the interspaces of the universe.

A thought in this substance produces the thing that is imaged in the thought.

Anyone can form things in thought and, by impressing that thought upon formless substance, can cause the thing to be created.

These basic statements are the essence of the creative process and form the foundation for all that follows.

SUMMARY

The desire for riches is simply our own capacity for larger life seeking fulfillment, so nature is friendly to your plans. Everything is naturally on your side. The universe desires you to have everything you want to have.

It's essential that your purpose should harmonize with the purpose that is in all. This means you must want real Life, not mere pleasure or sensual gratification.

You're not seeking anything that anyone else has; instead, you're causing what you want to be created from formless substance, and that supply is limitless.

Focus on that limitless supply and ignore any appearances to the contrary.

6. HOW RICHES COME TO YOU

———————— ⚜ ————————

When I say you don't have to drive sharp bargains, I'm not saying that you don't have to negotiate any deals at all or that you're above the necessity for doing business with others. I mean that you don't need to deal with them unfairly. *You don't have to get something for nothing; rather, you can give everyone more than you take.*

Giving More Than We Receive

You can't give everyone more in cash value than you receive, but you can give more in use value than the cash value of whatever you receive. The paper, ink, and other material in this book may not be worth the money you pay for it, but if the ideas suggested by it bring you thousands of dollars, you surely will not have been cheated by those who sold it to you; they've given you a great use value for a small cash value.

Let's suppose I have a tractor, worth thousands of dollars, and I put it on a boat and ship it up the Amazon to a village deep in the jungle. I offer it to the village chief, in return for a boatload of rare, medicinal herbs of no particular value to him. He will not take the tractor—he has no use for it. It's too big to fit on his footpaths, it's noisy, and there's no way to keep it fueled.

On the other hand, if I offer him a dozen steel machetes—one for each man in his village—and a sharpening stone, I have given him something useful in return for organizing the people of his village for a few days of gathering plants. This is a good bargain. He and his people will be able to do what they already do much more easily for years to come as a result of this trade.

When you give everyone more in use value than you receive in cash value, you're adding to the life of the world with every business transaction.

So, as you rise from the competitive mind to the creative mind, you can scan your business transactions, and if you're selling anyone anything that doesn't add more to their life than you received in exchange, you can afford to stop it.

You can also make your business do for your employees what this book is doing for you. If you have people working for you, the laws of economics require that you take from them more in cash value than you pay them in wages, but you can build your organization so that each employee who wishes to do so may advance a little every day. You can run your business like a ladder by which every employee who will take the trouble may climb to riches. Having set it up for them, given them the opportunity, and shown them it's there, you've done your part; it's their responsibility to take advantage of it.

You don't have to beat anybody in business to get rich. And if you're currently in a business that does beat people down, you must get out of it at once to obtain the riches you deserve.

Manifesting Resources

You're here to create your riches from the formless substance that permeates your environment, but what you desire isn't likely to instantly come into being before your eyes. Remember, thought impressed on substance begins to move in that substance according to pre-existing patterns of growth.

So, if you want a sewing machine, for instance, I'm not saying you're supposed to impress the thought of a sewing machine on thinking substance until the machine is formed without hands, right where you sit. Instead, if you want a sewing machine, hold the mental image of it with positive certainty that it's on its way to you. After once forming the thought, have the most absolute and unquestioning faith that the sewing machine is coming. Never think of it or speak of it in any other way than as being sure to arrive. Claim it as already yours.

It will be brought to you by the power of the supreme intelligence acting on the minds of people. If you live in Maine, it may be that someone will be brought from Texas or Japan to engage in some transaction that results in your getting what you want. If so, the whole matter will be as much to their advantage as it is to yours.

Don't forget for a moment that the thinking substance is through all, in all, communicating with all, and can influence all. The need in thinking substance for fuller life and better living has caused the creation of all the sewing machines that have already been made. It can cause the creation of millions more and will do so, whenever people set it in motion by their desire and faith and by acting in a certain way.

Experiencing Fuller Expression

You can certainly have a sewing machine in your house, and

it's just as certain that you can have any other thing that you want and will use for the advancement of your own life and the lives of others. So don't hesitate to ask for great things. Original substance wants to live all that is possible in you and wants you to have all that you can use and will use for living the most abundant life you can.

When you fully realize the fact that your desire for the possession of riches is at one with the desire of the supreme power for more complete expression, your faith becomes invincible.

Once I saw a little boy sitting at a piano, trying unsuccessfully to bring harmony out of the keys. I saw that he was frustrated by his inability to play real music. I asked him the cause of his distress, and he answered, "I can feel the music in me, but I can't make my hands go right." The music in him was the urge of original substance, containing all the possibilities of all life. All of music was seeking expression through the child.

So God, the one substance, is trying to live, do, and enjoy things through humanity. God is saying, "I want hands to build wonderful structures, to play divine harmonies, to paint glorious pictures. I want feet to run my errands, eyes to see my beauties, tongues to tell mighty truths and to sing marvelous songs." And so on.

All possibility is seeking expression through people. God wants those who can play music to have instruments and to have the means to cultivate their talents to the fullest extent. God wants those who can appreciate beauty to be able to surround themselves with beautiful things. God wants those who can discern truth to have every opportunity to travel and observe. God wants those who can appreciate dress to be beautifully clothed and those who can appreciate good food to be luxuriously fed.

God wants all these things because God enjoys and appreciates them. It's God who wants to play, and sing, and enjoy beauty, and proclaim truth, and wear fine clothes, and eat good foods. "God works in you to will and to do," said the apostle Paul.

The desire you feel for riches is the Infinite, seeking to express in and through you, just as the little boy at the piano.

"It is your Father's good pleasure to give you the kingdom," said Jesus (Luke 12:32). The author of Ecclesiastes, in 2:22–2:25, said, "There is nothing better for a man than to eat and drink, and to make his soul enjoy good in his endeavors . . . For God gives a man what is good in his sight: wisdom and knowledge and joy."

So don't hesitate to ask largely. Your part is to focus on that desire and express it to God.

This is a difficult point with most people. They're stuck in the old idea that poverty and self-sacrifice are pleasing to God. They think poverty is part of the plan, a necessity of nature. They have the idea that God has finished his work, made all that can be made, and that the majority of people must stay poor because there's not enough to go around. They hold so tightly to this error that they feel ashamed for what they already have. They try not to want more than a very modest competence, just enough to make them fairly comfortable.

I recall one student who was told that he must get in mind a clear picture of the things he desired, so that the creative thought of them might be impressed on formless substance. He was a very poor man, living in a rented house and having only what he earned from day to day, and he couldn't grasp the fact that all wealth was his.

So, after thinking the matter over, he decided that he might reasonably ask for a new rug for the floor of his best room and a coal stove to heat the house during the cold weather. Following the instructions given in this book, he obtained these things in a few months.

And then it dawned upon him that he hadn't asked enough.

He went through the house in which he lived and planned all the improvements he would like to make in it. He mentally added a bay window here and a room there until it was complete in his mind as his ideal home, and then he planned its furnishings. Holding the whole picture in his mind, he began living in the certain way and moving toward what he wanted.

He now owns the house and is rebuilding it to fit his mental image. And, with still larger faith, he's going on to get greater things.

It has come to him due to his faith, and so it is with you and with all of us.

SUMMARY

You don't have to get something for nothing; rather, you can give everyone more than you take. When you give everyone more in use value than you receive in cash value, you're adding to the life of the world with every business transaction.

You're here to create your riches from the formless substance that permeates your environment, but what you desire isn't likely to instantly come into being before your eyes. Remember, thought impressed on substance begins to move in that substance according to pre-existing patterns of growth.

God, as the one substance, is trying to live, do, and enjoy things through humanity. All possibility is seeking expression through people. When you fully realize the fact that your desire for the possession of riches is at one with the desire of the supreme power for more complete expression, your faith in its fulfillment becomes invincible.

7. GRATITUDE

❧

So FAR we've seen that the first step in getting rich is to impress the idea of your wants on the formless substance, and this is true, but doing so requires being in harmony with the formless intelligence.

Achieving this harmony is vitally important, so I want to talk about it at some length here and to give you instructions that will bring you into perfect unity of mind with the supreme power of the universe. The steps are simple:

1. Believe that there is one intelligent substance from which all things proceed.
2. Believe that this substance gives you everything you desire.
3. Relate to that intelligent substance through a feeling of deep and profound gratitude.

The whole process of mental adjustment and attunement can be summed up in that one last word: *Gratitude*.

Many people who do everything else right stay in poverty due to their lack of gratitude. Having received a gift, they cut the wires that connect them with the source by failing to acknowledge that gift.

It's easy to understand that the nearer we live to the source of riches, the more riches we will receive, and it's easy also to understand that someone who is always grateful lives in closer touch with that source than one who never offers thankful acknowledgment. The more gratefully we fix our minds on the supreme source when good things come to us, the more good things we will receive, and the more rapidly they will come.

The reason for this is simply that *an attitude of gratitude draws the mind closer to the source from which all blessings come.* Jesus always gave thanks first. The Koran teaches that God *(Allah)* "of His mercy has appointed for you night and day, so you may rest and so you may seek His bounty, and so that, happily, you may be thankful . . . whoever gives thanks does so for the good of his soul" (28:73; 31:12).

If the thought that gratitude brings your whole mind into closer harmony with the creative energies of the universe is new to you, consider it, and you'll see it's true. The good things you already have came to you along specific pathways according to laws that can be counted on. Gratitude leads your mind out along the ways by which those things came and opens the flow for further blessings.

It also keeps you in close harmony with creative thought and prevents you from falling into competitive thought. Gratitude alone can keep you looking toward the all-providing source, preventing you from falling into the error of thinking that the supply might be limited, which is an idea that can wipe out your hopes.

The Law of Gratitude

There is a law of gratitude, and it's absolutely necessary that you observe this law to get the results you seek.

The Law of Gratitude is based on the natural principle that "action and reaction are always equal and in opposite directions."[4] This means that an action leading outward is always followed by a reaction coming inward. So the action of expressing thankful praise to the supreme intelligence must lead to an equal reaction toward us. *Our gratitude liberates an energy within us that immediately expands into the formless substance, where it is instantly returned to us in kind.*

If your gratitude is strong and constant, the response of formless substance will be strong and continuous, and the things you want will always move toward you. Notice the grateful attitude Jesus maintained, how he always seemed to be saying, "I thank you, Father, that you have heard me."

You can't exercise much power without gratitude, for gratitude is what keeps you connected with power.

The Benefits of Gratitude

But the value of gratitude is not just in getting you more blessings in the future; without gratitude, you can't keep from becoming dissatisfied with things as they are. The moment you stop feeling grateful for your blessings and start to feel dissatisfied with things as they are, you begin to lose ground.

The reason is simple. When dissatisfied, you only see what is not okay—what's broken or dirty, what's not right in your world, and your thoughts take the form of these things. Then you transmit these forms or mental images

---

4 Sir Isaac Newton applied this long-known metaphysical principle to physical objects in the 1600s, when he developed his "Laws of Motion," saying "For every action, there is an equal and opposite reaction" (Newton's Third Law).

to the formless, and more of what you don't want starts to come to you.

To focus attention on the inferior or undesirable is to become inferior and to find yourself surrounded with inferior or undesirable things. On the other hand, to fix your attention on the best is to surround yourself with the best and to become the best. The creative power within us makes us into the image of whatever we give our attention to. We, too, are made of thinking substance, and thinking substance always takes the form of the thought it experiences.

The grateful mind is constantly fixed upon the highest and best; therefore, it tends to become the best. Taking the form or character of the best, it will receive the best.

Another benefit is increased faith. Faith is born of gratitude. The grateful mind continually perceives good things, which becomes expectation of more of the same, which becomes faith: a deep understanding and knowledge. So every outgoing wave of grateful thanksgiving increases faith. Someone who has no feeling of gratitude cannot long retain a living faith, and without a living faith you can't get rich by the creative method, as we shall see in the following chapters.

Gratitude in all Things

It's essential, then, to develop the habit of being grateful for every good thing that comes to you and to give thanks continually.

And *because all things have contributed to your advancement, they're all good; so you need to include all things in your gratitude.*

Don't waste a lot of time thinking or talking about the shortcomings or wrong actions of those in power. Their organization of the world has created your opportunity; all you get really comes to you because of them. Don't rage against corrupt politicians. If it were not for politicians, we should fall into anarchy, and your opportunities would be greatly lessened.

God, the intelligence of infinite substance, has worked a long time and very patiently to bring us to where we are in industry and government, and that work continues. There's no doubt that the forces of ongoing development will do away with greedy corporate executives[5] and politicians as soon as they can be spared, but in the meantime, they're all very necessary.

Remember that they're all helping to arrange the lines of transmission along which your riches will come to you, and be grateful. This will bring you into harmonious relations with the good in everything, and the good in everything will move toward you.

SUMMARY

The more gratefully we fix our minds on the Supreme when good things come to us, the more good things we receive, and the more rapidly they come. This is simply because the attitude of gratitude draws us closer to the source from which the blessings come.

Without gratitude you can't keep from becoming dissatisfied with things as they are. The moment you stop feeling grateful for your blessings and let your mind dwell with dissatisfaction upon things as they are, you begin to lose ground.

---

5 The author's original text said, "plutocrats, trust magnates, captains of industry," all of which, as he predicted when he wrote in 1910, are now gone . . . hmm.

The grateful mind continually perceives good things, and that continual perception becomes expectation of more of the same, which becomes faith: a deep understanding and knowledge.

Because all things have contributed to your advancement, they're all good; so you need to include all things in your gratitude. Don't waste time thinking or talking about the shortcomings or wrong actions of those in power . . . they're all helping to arrange the lines of transmission along which your riches will come to you.

8. THINKING IN THE CERTAIN WAY

———— ⚜ ————

IF YOU'LL turn back to Chapter 6 and reread the story of the man who formed a mental image of his house, you'll get a fair idea of the first step toward getting rich.

Be Clear and Precise

You must form a clear and definite mental picture of what you want; you can't transmit an idea into the substance unless you have it clearly yourself. You must have it before you can give it, and many people fail to impress thinking substance because they have only a vague and misty idea of the things they want to do, have, or become.

It's not enough to have a general desire for wealth to do good in the world. Everybody has that desire. It's not enough to wish to travel, see things, live more, etc. Everybody has those desires also.

If you were going to send a message to a friend, you wouldn't send a list of the letters in the alphabet and expect him to construct the message for himself, nor would you take words at random from the dictionary. You would send a coherent sentence that meant something to both of you.

In the same way, when you try to impress your desires upon the thinking substance, remember to make a coherent statement. You must know what you want and be specific and definite. You can never get rich nor start the creative power into action by sending out unformed longings and vague desires.

Go over your desires, just as the man I have described went over his house. See just what you are ready to receive, and get a clear mental picture of it as you wish it to look when you get it.

Holding the Image

Then you must have that clear mental picture, or vision, continually in your mind. As the sailor has in mind the port toward which he is sailing the ship, you must keep your face toward your vision all the time. You must no more lose sight of it than the helmsman loses sight of the compass.

Spend as much of your leisure time as you can contemplating your picture. You don't need to take exercises in concentration, set apart special times for prayer and affirmation, "go into the silence," or anything else of the kind. Some of these activities are well enough for their own purposes, but *all you need to accomplish your goal is to know what you want and to want it badly enough that it will stay in your thoughts.*

The more clear and definite you make your picture and the more you imagine it, bringing out all its delightful details, the stronger your desire will be. And the stronger your desire, the easier it will be to hold your mind fixed on the picture of what you want. It's the things we don't really care about that take an effort to focus on.

Remember, the methods in this book are for people whose desire for riches is strong enough to overcome mental laziness and the love of ease to make them work. So unless you really want to get rich and fulfill your potential, with a desire strong enough to hold your thoughts directed to your vision as steadily as the magnetic pole holds the needle of the compass, it will hardly be worthwhile for you to try to carry out the instructions given in this book.

With Intention and Faith

Something more is necessary, however, than merely to see the picture clearly. If that's all you do, you're just a dreamer, with little or no power to accomplish your vision. Behind your clear vision must be the real intention to realize it, to bring it into tangible expression. And behind this intention must be an invincible and unwavering faith that the thing is already yours, at hand, and you only have to take possession of it.

"Whatever you ask for in prayer, believing that you receive them, you shall have," said Jesus (Mark 11:24–25). We must ask, believing that it's already ours, before we can actually possess what we've asked for.

So contemplate your vision until it's clear and distinct, then take the mental attitude of owning everything in that picture. In your imagination, start enjoying the things you desire. Take possession of it all in your mind, in the full faith that it's actually yours now. Hold to this mental ownership. Live in the new house, mentally, until it takes form around you physically. See the things you desire as if they were actually around you all the time. See yourself owning and using them. Make use of them in imagination just as you will use them when they are your tangible possessions.

Don't waver for an instant in the faith that it is real.

And remember what was said in Chapter 7 about gratitude: be as thankful for it while you're imagining it as you expect to be when it has taken form. Those who can sincerely thank God for the things they own only in imagination have real faith. They will get rich. They will cause the creation of whatever they want.

Unceasing, not Repeating

You don't need to pray repeatedly for things you want. It's not necessary to tell God about it every day. Your part is to intelligently formulate your desire for the things that will give you a larger life and to arrange those desires into a coherent whole, then to impress this whole desire upon the formless substance, which has the power and the will to bring you what you want.

You don't make this impression by repeating strings of words; you make it by imagining with all of your senses and holding the vision with unshakable intention to attain it and with steadfast faith that you will attain it. Prayer is not answered according to the faith you hold while you're talking, but according to the faith maintained while you're working.

You can't impress the mind of God by having a special Sabbath day set apart to ask for what you want, and then forgetting the source of your gifts during the rest of the week. You can't impress the Father by having special hours to go into your closet and pray if you then dismiss the matter from your mind until the hour of prayer comes again.

Oral prayer is fine and has its effect, especially upon your own mind, by clarifying your vision and strengthening your faith, but your oral requests don't get you what you want. In order to get rich you don't need a "sweet hour of prayer"; you need to "pray without ceasing."

And by prayer I mean holding steadily to your vision, with the clear intention to bring about its creation into solid form and with doubt-free faith that you are doing so.

Believing That You Receive Them

Once you've clearly formed your vision, your success depends on receiving.

It's useful to make an oral statement addressing the Supreme in gratitude. Then, from that moment on you must, in your imagination, receive what you ask for. Live in the new house, wear the fine clothes, ride in the automobile, go on the journey, and confidently plan greater journeys.

Think and speak of all the things you've asked for as if you actually already owned them. Imagine your environment and finances exactly as you want them, and live all the time in that mental environment and financial condition until and while you see them take shape.

Make sure, though, that you're not doing this as a dreamer and castle-builder. Hold to the faith that the imaginary is now being realized and to your intention to experience it. Remember that faith and intention in the use of the imagination are what make the difference between the scientist and the dreamer.

And having learned this fact, it's time to learn the proper use of will.

SUMMARY

You must form a clear and definite mental picture of what you want. You can't transmit an idea into the substance unless you have it yourself; many people fail to impress thinking substance because they have only a vague and misty idea of the things they want to do, have, or become.

Then you must have that clear mental picture continually in your mind; all you need to accomplish your goal is to know what you want and to want it badly enough that it will stay in your thoughts.

Behind your clear vision must be the real intention to realize it, to bring it into tangible expression. And behind this intention must be an invincible and unwavering faith that the thing is already yours, at hand, and you have only to take possession of it.

When you've formed the vision, it's useful to make an oral statement, addressing the Supreme in gratitude. Then, from that moment on you must, in your imagination, receive what you ask for.

9. HOW TO USE THE WILL

———————— ⚜ ————————

IN NO way whatsoever does the science of getting rich require you to apply power or force to any other person. You truly don't need to try to apply the power of your will to anything outside of yourself to get rich.

So don't try to project your will, your thoughts, or your mind outwardly to act on things or people in your environment. Keep your mind at home. Believe me, it can accomplish much more there than elsewhere.

You have no right to do so anyway. It's wrong to impose your will on others in order to get them to do what you want. It's as wrong to coerce people by mental power as it is to coerce them by physical power. If compelling people by physical force to do things for you reduces them to slavery, compelling them by mental means does exactly the same thing; the only difference is the method. If taking things from people by physical force is robbery, taking things by mental force is also robbery. There's no difference in principle.

You don't even have a right to use your will power upon another person "for their own good," since you can't ever really know what is best for anybody else.

You don't need to apply your will to compel things to come to you either. That would be trying to coerce God, which is both foolish and useless: you don't have to try to compel God to give you good things any more than you have to use your willpower to make the sun rise. There's really no need to do so. The infinite substance that permeates the universe is friendly to you, and is more anxious to give you what you want than you are to get it.

This means you don't even have to use your willpower to conquer any unfriendly power or to make stubborn and rebellious forces do your bidding, since the power of the friendly infinite substance is everywhere, so can be the only power that affects you.

In fact, any attempt to impose your will on anyone or anything outside of you will only tend to defeat your purpose.

Managing Our Thoughts and Actions
To get rich, you need only to use your willpower on yourself.

When you know what to think and do, you use your will to compel yourself to think and do those things. Use your will to keep yourself thinking and acting in the certain way outlined here. That's the only legitimate use of the will in getting what you want: holding yourself to the right course.

Use your mind to form a mental image of what you want and to hold that vision with faith and intention, and use your will to keep your mind working in the certain way I've been describing in this book.

Holding the Intention
The more steadily and continuously you hold to your faith and intention, the sooner you'll get rich because you'll be

making only *positive* impressions upon substance, without neutralizing or offsetting them by negative impressions. Then the picture of your desires, held with faith and intention, is taken up by the formless, and permeates it—throughout the universe, for all we know.

As the impression of your idea spreads, all things are set moving toward its realization. Every living thing, every inanimate thing, and even the things not yet created begin to move toward bringing into being that which you are intending. All harmonious forces begin to be exerted in that direction. All the components begin to move toward you. The minds of people everywhere are influenced toward doing the things necessary to fulfill your desires, and, without even realizing they're doing so, they go to work for you.

You can check all this by starting a negative impression in the formless substance. Doubt or unbelief is as certain to start a movement away from you as faith and intention are to start one toward you. It's by not understanding this that most people fail. Every moment you spend paying attention to doubts and fears, every hour you spend worrying, every hour your soul wrestles with unbelief sets a current away from you in the intelligent substance.

All the promises are "unto them that believe" and unto them only. This is why Jesus was so insistent on that point.

Since belief is all-important, you need to guard your thoughts, and as your beliefs will be shaped to a very great extent by the things you observe and think about, you should carefully limit what you give your attention to.

It's here that the will comes into use, for it's with your will that you focus your attention.

Helping the Poor, the Sick, and the Needy

If you want to become rich, you must not study poverty.

Things are not brought into being by thinking about their opposites. Studying and thinking about disease does not achieve health. Studying and thinking about sin does not promote righteousness. And no one ever got rich by studying poverty and thinking about poverty.

Medicine, as a science of disease, has increased disease; religion, as a science of sin, has promoted sin; and economics as a study of poverty will fill the world with wretchedness and want.

So, don't talk about poverty, investigate it, or even concern yourself with it. Never mind what its causes are; you have nothing to do with them. What concerns you is the cure.

Don't spend your time in so-called charitable work or charity movements. In spite of all good intentions, most charity only tends to perpetuate the wretchedness it aims to relieve.[6] And you can't hold the mental image that can make you rich if you fill your mind with pictures of poverty and all its attendant ills.

I'm not saying you should be hardhearted or unkind and refuse to hear the cry of need, but to accomplish your goal you must not try to eradicate poverty in any of the conventional ways.

Don't read books or papers that describe the misery of life in the slums, the horrors of child labor, and so on. Don't read anything that fills your mind with gloomy images of want and suffering.

You can't help the poor at all by knowing about these things, and the widespread knowledge of them has not helped to do away with poverty. Get rich. That's the best

6 This principle has also been stated as, "Whatever we resist, persists."

way you can help the poor. Put poverty behind you; put everything about it behind you and make good.

You're not deserting the poor in their misery when you refuse to allow your mind to be filled with pictures of that misery. What tends to do away with poverty is not putting pictures of poverty into your mind but getting pictures of wealth, abundance, and possibility into the minds of the poor. Poverty can be done away with, not by increasing the number of well-to-do people who think about poverty, but by increasing the number of poor people who intend with faith to get rich.

Some people remain in poverty because they don't know that there is wealth for them, and these people can best be taught by showing them the way to affluence through your own presence and practice. Others are poor because, while they feel that there is a way out, they are unwilling to put forth the mental effort necessary to find that way and travel it. For these, the very best thing you can do is to motivate them by showing them the happiness that comes from being rightly rich.

Others still are poor because, while they have some notion of this science, they've become so lost in the maze of theories offered them that they can't see which road to take. They try a mixture of many systems and fail in all. For these, again, the very best thing to do is to show the simplest way with your own presence and practice.

The poor don't need charity; they need inspiration. Charity only sends them a loaf of bread to keep them alive in their wretchedness or gives them an entertainment to make them forget for an hour or two. But inspiration can cause them to rise out of their misery. If you want to help the poor, demonstrate to them that they can become rich.

Prove it by getting rich yourself.

You're not being hardhearted or unfeeling when you refuse to pity poverty, see poverty, read about poverty, think or talk about it, or listen to those who talk about it. Use your willpower to keep your mind *off* the subject of poverty and to keep it fixed with faith and intention *on* the vision of what you want and are creating.

SUMMARY

The science of getting rich does not require you to apply power or force or "mind control" on any other person or thing; in fact, to try to do so delays your progress.

Things are not brought into being by thinking about their opposites. If you want to become rich, you must not study poverty; the best way you can help the poor is to get rich and become an inspiration, giving them a model to focus on.

The more steadily and continuously you hold to your faith and intention, the sooner you'll get rich because you'll be making only positive impressions upon substance, without neutralizing or offsetting them by negative impressions.

Use your willpower to keep your mind off the subject of poverty and to keep it fixed with faith and intention on the vision of what you are creating.

10. FURTHER USE
OF THE WILL

⸰⚜⸰

THERE'S NO way to retain a true and clear vision of wealth and fulfillment if you're paying attention to opposing images, whether they be in the world around you or in your imagination.

Avoiding Distracting Images and Ideas

Don't talk about your past financial troubles if you have had them. Don't think of them at all. Don't tell of the poverty of your parents or the hardships of your early life. To do any of these things is to mentally class yourself with the poor for the time being, and it slows, or even stops, the movement of things in your direction. Put poverty and all things relating to poverty completely behind you.

Whenever you think or speak of those who are poor, think and speak of them as those who are becoming rich, as those who are to be congratulated rather than pitied. Then they and others will catch the inspiration and begin to search for the way out.

And read only the most optimistic comments on the world's news, those in harmony with your picture. Don't read books that tell you that the world is coming to an end, and don't read the writing of detractors and naysayers who tell you it's going to the devil. The world is not going to the devil; it's going to God. It's a wonderful becoming!

True, there may be a good many disagreeable things going on, but what's the use of studying them when they surely are passing away and when the study of them only tends to slow their passing and keep them with us?

Why spend your time and attention on things that are being displaced through evolutionary development, when you can only help that development by applying the principles of this science and more than filling your position in the world?

No matter how seemingly horrible the conditions in other places may be, you waste your time and destroy your own chances for fulfillment and effectiveness by dwelling on them.

Instead, interest yourself in the whole world's becoming rich. Think of the riches the world is coming into instead of the poverty it's growing out of, and bear in mind that the only way you can help the world grow rich is by growing rich yourself, through the creative method, not the competitive one.

Give your attention wholly to riches. Do not focus on any form of poverty, lack, or distress.

Serving God and Humanity

Even though I say that you are to give all of your time and thought to riches, I'm in no way suggesting that you are to be sordid or mean. To become really rich is the noblest aim you can have in life, for it includes everything else. *The very best thing you can do for the whole world is to make the most of yourself.*

If you aren't completely healthy, you'll find that being free of financial concerns will reduce stress and allow you the time and means to restore your body to full health and capacity. If you seek spiritual development, you'll find that moral and spiritual greatness are possible when you no longer have to struggle for means of existence. If you seek satisfying and fulfilling relationships, you'll discover that love flourishes where there are opportunities to enjoy the delights of this world and explore new possibilities together. All that is possible in the way of greatness, service, and high achievement, comes by way of getting rich because all is made possible by the use of things.[7]

You can serve God and humanity in no more effective way than by getting rich; that is, if you get rich by the creative method and not by the competitive one. People must be taught to become rich by creation, not by competition. To the competitive mind, the struggle to get rich is a godless scramble for power over others, but when we come into the creative mind, all this is changed. Anyone who gets rich by competition knocks down the ladder by which he rises, and so keeps others down, but everyone who gets rich by creation opens a way for thousands to follow—and inspires them to do so.

The only way poverty and related distress will ever be banished from this world is by getting a large and constantly

---

7 One of the greatest men ever to live was Mohandas K. Gandhi, called *Mahatma*, or "Great Soul," because of the way he embodied spiritual principles. He had only begun his work when Waddles was writing this book, but by the 1940s, this "little brown man," who lived the life of the poorest Hindu,

increasing number of people to practice the methods described in this book. An ounce of doing is worth a pound of theorizing.

Sticking to One Effective Path

Another thing: with this book, you've accepted a certain theory of the universe as being correct and are resting all your hopes of happiness on its being correct. What can you gain by paying attention to conflicting theories?

I assert that this book gives, in detail, all the principles of the science of getting rich, and if that's true, you don't need to read any other book on the subject.

This may sound narrow and egotistical, but consider: there's only one shortest distance between two points. Likewise, there's only one way to think effectively: the way that takes the most direct and simple route to the goal. No one has yet formulated a briefer or less complex system than the one set forth here. It's been stripped of all nonessentials, and it works.

If you do try to mix this approach with others, you'll begin to have doubts and to be uncertain and wavering in your thoughts and images, and then you will begin to make failures.

Also, don't dabble in spiritualism, mediumship, or related studies. Perhaps the dead still live and are near, but if they are, let them alone; mind your own business. Wherever the spirits of the dead may be, they have their own work to do, and we have no right to interfere with them. We can't help them, and it's very doubtful whether they can help us

---

had brought the British Empire to its knees. It cost about $50,000 each month in today's dollars to support Gandhi's work, causing one of his backers to say, "It takes a lot of money to keep Gandhi in poverty." The film, *Gandhi*, is a very effective illustration of these principles.

or whether we have any right to trespass upon their time if they can. Let the dead and the hereafter alone, and focus on solving your own problem: getting rich and fulfilling your potential. If you begin to rely on the words of mediums, you will start mental crosscurrents that will surely bring your hopes to shipwreck.

So when you begin this process, lay all other methods aside. Put them completely out of your mind.

Read this book every day. Keep it with you. Commit it to memory, and don't waste your time on other systems and theories.

After you've become rich and are sure you've accomplished what you set out to, then you may study other systems as much as you please.

For now, remember the basic principles of *this* system:

There is a thinking stuff from which all things are made and which, in its original state, permeates, penetrates, and fills the interspaces of the universe.

A thought in this substance produces the thing that is imaged in the thought.

People can form images in their thoughts and, by impressing those thoughts upon the formless substance, can cause the thing they think about to be created.

To do this, you must shift from the competitive mind to the creative mind. You must form a clear mental picture of the things you desire and hold this vision in your thoughts with the fixed intention to receive those things and the unwavering faith that you will receive them.

SUMMARY

Put poverty and all things relating to poverty completely behind you. Whenever you think or speak of those who are poor, think and speak of them as those who are becoming rich, as those who are to be congratulated rather than pitied.

There may be many disagreeable conditions, but studying them only tends to slow their passing. You hasten their removal only by promoting social and economic development. You waste your time and destroy your own chances by dwelling on them.

Instead, interest yourself in the whole world's becoming rich. You can serve God and humanity in no more effective way than by getting rich; that is, if you get rich by the creative method and not by the competitive one.

Whoever would get rich must close their mind against anything or anybody that could shake their intention, dim their vision, or weaken their faith.

II. ACTING IN THE
CERTAIN WAY

————————— ⚜ —————————

By THOUGHT, you can cause the gold in the hearts of the mountains to be impelled toward you, but it will not mine itself, refine itself, coin itself, and come rolling along the roads, seeking its way into your pocket.

Under the impelling power of the supreme spirit, someone will be led to mine the gold for you. Other people's business transactions will be directed, so the gold will be brought to you. And you must arrange your own business affairs, so you can receive it when it arrives. Your thought makes all things, animate and inanimate, work to bring you what you desire, but your personal activity must be set up, so you can rightly receive what you desire when it reaches you. You are not to take it as charity or to steal it. *You must give everyone more in use value than they give you in cash value.*

The scientific use of thought consists of:

forming a clear and distinct mental image of what you want,

holding fast to your intention to get what you want, and

realizing with grateful faith that you do get what you want.

Don't try to project your thought in any mysterious or magical way, with the idea of having it go out and do things for you. It's a waste of effort that can weaken your power to think clearly.

The function of thought in getting rich is fully explained in the preceding chapters: your faith and intention positively impress your vision upon formless substance, which has the same desire for more life that you have, and this vision, received from you, sets all the creative forces at work in and through their regular channels of action, directed toward you. It's not your job to guide or supervise the creative process; *all you have to do is retain your vision, stick to your intention, and maintain your faith and gratitude.*

The Necessity for Action
Thought is the force that causes the creative power to work for us. And while it's true that thinking in a certain way will bring riches to you, you must not rely upon thought alone, ignoring action. That's the iceberg too many otherwise scientific thinkers are shipwrecked upon—the failure to connect thought with action.

So, don't impress your creative impulse in original substance and then sit down and wait for results. If you do, you'll never get them. Your wallet is not likely to suddenly fill itself with no effort on your part, just as the sewing machine isn't likely to suddenly appear in front of you.

Humanity hasn't yet reached the stage of development (assuming we ever will) in which anyone can create something directly from formless substance without relying on natural processes or the work of human hands.[8] We must not only think, but must supplement our thought with action.

But you must act in a certain way, so you can accept what is yours when it comes to you and can put the things you have in your vision in their proper places as they arrive.

You can see the truth of this. When things reach you, they'll be in the hands of others who will ask an equivalent value for them. And you can only get what is yours by giving them what is rightfully theirs.

This is the crucial point in the science of getting rich— right here, where thought and personal action meet.

Too many people, consciously or unconsciously, set the creative forces in action by the strength and persistence of their desires but remain poor because they don't provide for the reception of the thing they want when it comes.

By thought, whatever you focus on is brought to you. By action, you receive it.

Acting Now

Whatever your action is to be, you must act *now*. You cannot act in the past, and it's essential to the clarity of your mental vision that you dismiss the past from your mind. You cannot act in the future; the future isn't here yet. Besides, you can't tell how you will want to act in any future contingency until that contingency has arrived.

Act now. There's never any time but now, and there never

---

8 While certain Buddhist monks, Hindu gurus, and shamans appear to have developed this capacity, even they must act in certain ways in order to manifest the material they intend.

will be any time but now. If you are ever to get ready to receive what you want, you must begin *now*. If you're not in the
right business or the right environment now, don't persuade
yourself that you have to wait until you get into the right
business or environment to act. And don't spend your time in
the present thinking about possible future emergencies; have
faith in your ability to meet any emergency when it arrives.

Put your whole mind into present action. If you act in
the present with your mind on the future, your present action will be with a divided mind and will not be effective.

And your action, whatever it is, can only be in your present business or employment, with the people and things in
your present environment. You can't act where you are not,
you can't act where you have been, and you can't act where
you are going to be. You can act only where you are, now.

Don't worry whether yesterday's work was done well or
poorly; do today's work well.

Don't try to do tomorrow's work now; you'll have plenty
of time to do it then.

Don't try to use telepathy or project your will to act on
people or things that are elsewhere, out of your reach.

Don't wait for a change of environment before you act;
get a change of environment by your action. You can act
within the environment that you're in now in ways that will
cause you to be transferred to a better environment. Hold
the vision of yourself in the better environment with faith
and intention, but act within your present environment with
all your heart, all your strength, and all your mind.

Don't spend any time daydreaming about what might
happen if you get what you want; hold the one vision of
what you want, and act *now*.

Don't try to project your thought into space and rely

upon it to get you another job; it will probably fail to do so.

Don't look around, seeking some new thing to do or some strange, unusual, or remarkable action to perform as a first step toward getting rich. *It's most likely that you'll be doing, at least for some time, the same things you've been doing, but you begin now to do them in a way that will make you rich.*

Don't feel discouraged or sorry for yourself because you're in the wrong place. If you're in some line of work that you feel isn't the right one for you, don't wait until you get into the right one before you begin to act. Nobody is so misplaced that they can't find their right place simply by more than filling their current one.

Hold the vision of yourself in the right place, with the intention to get into it and the faith that you are getting into it, but *act* in your present place. Use your present position as the means for getting a better one, and use your present environment as the means for getting into a better one.

Your vision of the right position, if held with faith and intention, will cause the supreme power to move the right position toward you. And your action, if performed in the certain way described here, will cause you to move toward that position.

In closing this chapter, we review our basic principles, adding to our list:

There is a thinking stuff from which all things are made and which, in its original state, permeates, penetrates, and fills the interspaces of the universe.

A thought in this substance produces the thing that is imaged in the thought.

Everyone can form images in their thoughts and, by impressing those thoughts on the formless substance, can cause the thing they think about to be created.

To do this, they must shift from the competitive mind to the creative mind. They must form a clear mental picture of the things they desire and hold this vision in their thoughts with the fixed intention to receive those things and the unwavering faith that they do receive them, closing their mind to anything that may tend to shake their intention, dim their vision, or quench their faith.

To receive what they want when it comes, they must act now with the people and things in their present environment.

SUMMARY

By thought, the thing you want is brought to you. By action, you receive it.

Your action, whatever it is, will probably be in your present business or employment, with the people and things in your present environment. You can't act where you are not, you can't act where you have been, and you can't act where you are going to be. You can act only where you are.

If you're in some line of work that you feel isn't the right one for you, don't wait until you get into the right one before you begin to act. Hold the vision of yourself in the right place, with the intention to get into it and the faith that you are getting into it, but act in your present place.

12. EFFECTIVE ACTION

⸎

To PUT this system to work, you must use your thought as directed in previous chapters and begin to do what you can do where you are now. More, you must do all that you can do where you are.

The Process of Development

You can move up in the world only by being more than your present position requires, and no one can be greater than their position who doesn't get the work done. The world progresses only when people have more than filled the requirements of their present positions.

Conversely, those who don't fill their positions slow the progress of the world. No society can advance if everyone does less than their positions call for; social development is guided by mental development. If nobody quite fills his or her present position, you can see that everything slides downward. Those who don't quite fill their positions are deadweights in society, in government, business, the military, and industry. Others must carry them, at a great expense to all. Degeneration of the whole is the only possible result.

In the animal world, evolution is the result of excess life. When an organism has more life than can be expressed in the functions of its niche, it develops organs for a larger niche, and a new species is originated. There never would have been new species if there hadn't been organisms that more than filled their places.

The law is exactly the same for your getting rich: your moving to a larger niche depends on your applying this principle in your own life.

Getting Things Done

Every day is either a successful day or a day of failures, and it's the successful days that get you what you want. If every day is filled with failures, you can never get rich, but *if every day is a success, you can't fail to get rich.*

If there's something that may be done today and you don't get it done, you've failed so far as that thing is concerned, and the consequences may be more disastrous than you imagine.

You can never foresee the full results of even the most trivial act. You don't know all the forces that have been set moving in your behalf. Much may be depending on your doing some simple act, which may be the very act meant to open the door to great possibilities. You can never know all the combinations that supreme intelligence is making for you in the world of things and of human affairs. Your neglect or failure to do some small thing may seriously delay the arrival of what you want.

So do, every day, all that can be done that day.

However, *you are not to overwork or rush blindly into your business* in an effort to do the greatest possible number of things in the shortest possible time. You are not to try to do tomorrow's work today or do a week's work in a day. It's really not the number of things you do, but the *effectiveness* of each separate action that counts.

Powerful, Effective Action

Just as every action is, in itself, either a success or a failure, every action is either effective or ineffective. Effective action completes the task using the resources at hand and sets the foundation for further possibilities. Ineffective action is busying oneself in the process without getting the job done, using far more resources than the job would normally require or missing important opportunities.

The cause of failure is doing too many things ineffectively and not doing enough things effectively. Every ineffective action is a failure, and if you spend your life doing things ineffectively, your whole life will be a failure. The more things you do, the worse for you, if all your actions are ineffective.

On the other hand, every effective action is a success in itself, and if every action you take is an effective one, your whole life must be a success. And if it's possible for you to make each action effective, you see again that getting rich is reduced to an exact science, like mathematics.

This is the point where the people who separate mental power from personal action fail. They use the power of mind in one place and time, and they act in another way in another place and time. So their actions are not successful in themselves; too many of them are ineffective.

You can see that if you took no ineffective actions and a sufficient number of effective actions, you would become rich. The question then is whether you can make each separate action a success in itself. And this you can certainly do.

You can make each action a success, because the supreme power is working with you, and supreme power cannot fail. The omnipotence of infinite substance is at your service, and to be effective in every action, you only have to put that power into it.[9]

Every action can be made powerful and effective by holding your vision while you are doing it and putting the whole power of your faith and intention into it. So, just as every action is either effective or ineffective, every action is either powerful or weak, and when every action is powerfully effective, you are acting in the way that will make you rich.

Cumulative Progress

If all-power goes into every action, no matter how commonplace, every action will be a success in itself. And since it is the nature of things that every success opens the way to other successes, your progress towards what you want and the progress of what you want towards you speeds up tremendously.

Remember that successful action is cumulative in its results. Since the desire for more life is inherent in all things, when people begin to move toward larger life, more things are attracted to them, and the influence of their intention is multiplied.

So do, every day, all that you can do that day, and be effective in every action.

---

9 In *Creativity in Business*, Michael Ray and Rochelle Myers describe a study done at the Stanford business school which found that successful entrepreneurs were most effective when they did the things that were energizing, effortless, and enjoyable, delegating or avoiding the rest.

Building the Energy of the Vision

In saying that you must hold your vision while you undertake every action, however trivial or commonplace, I'm not saying you must see the vision distinctly at all times in its smallest details. Use your time off to focus on the details of your vision and to contemplate them until they are firmly fixed in your memory. Contemplate your image until your consciousness is so full of it that you can grasp it instantly.

For quick results, spend practically all your spare time in this practice. Continuous contemplation of your vision fixes the picture of what you want, even to the smallest details, so firmly upon your mind and so completely transfers it to the formless substance that you need only to think of it for an instant to bring it forth. You'll become so excited about the possibility that the slightest thought of it will energize your whole being. It will stimulate your faith and intention and bring forth your best effort.[10]

Again, let's repeat our basic statements, and add a new closing statement to bring it to the point we've reached.

There is a thinking stuff from which all things are made and which, in its original state, permeates, penetrates, and fills the interspaces of the universe.

A thought in this substance produces the thing that is imaged in the thought.

Everyone can form things in their thoughts and, by impressing thoughts upon the formless substance, can cause the thing they think about to be created.

---

10 The movie *The Castaway* is a perfect illustration of this principle at work.

In order to do this, people must pass from the competitive to the creative mind; they must form a clear mental picture of the things they want; and they must do, with faith and intention, everything that can be done each day, effectively.

SUMMARY

You can move up in the world only by being more than your present position requires, and no one can be greater than their position who doesn't get the work done.

Do, every day, all that can be done that day, but don't overwork or rush blindly into your business trying to do the greatest possible number of things in the shortest possible time. Don't try to do tomorrow's work today or do a week's work in a day. It's not the number of things you do but the effectiveness of each separate action that counts as success.

Successful action is cumulative in its results. Since every success opens the way to other successes, your progress toward what you want and the progress of what you want toward you speeds up tremendously with every success.

Continuous contemplation of your vision fixes the picture of what you want, even to the smallest details, so firmly upon your mind and so completely transfers it to the formless substance that, in your working hours, you need only to think of it to stimulate your faith and intention and bring forth your best effort.

13. THE RIGHT BUSINESS

⚜

SUCCESS, IN any particular business, depends in part on having developed the talents and abilities required in that business.

Without musical ability, no one can succeed as a teacher of music. Without well developed mechanical abilities, no one can achieve great success as a mechanic or technician. Without tact and the ability to manage and keep track of accounts, no one can succeed in sales.

But having the required capabilities for your particular vocation doesn't guarantee getting rich. There are musicians who have remarkable talent and yet remain poor. There are electricians, carpenters, and technicians of all sorts who have excellent mechanical ability but don't get rich.

The different abilities are tools. We have to have good tools, but we also have to use the tools the right way. One person can take a sharp saw, a square, a good plane, and related tools and build a handsome piece of furniture. Another can take the same tools and set to work to duplicate the article, but the product will be a mess if he or she doesn't know how to use those good tools effectively.

The various faculties of your mind are the tools you must use to make you rich. So it will be easier for you to succeed if you're in a business for which you have the right mental tools.

Desire and Talent

Generally speaking, you'll do best in the business for which you are naturally best fitted, using your strongest abilities. But there are limitations to this statement: the talents you were born with do not irrevocably fix your vocation.

You can get rich in any business, since, if you don't have the right talent, you can develop it. You'll simply have to build your tools as you go along, instead of relying on the ones you were born with. It's easier for you to succeed in a vocation that you've already developed the talents for, but because you can develop any rudimentary talent, and there's no talent that everyone doesn't have at some level, you can succeed in any vocation.

In fact, you can do whatever you want to do, and it is your right and privilege to follow the business or vocation that will be most congenial and pleasant. You're not obliged to do what you don't like to do and should not do it except as part of the process of getting to do the thing you want to do (going to college, for example).

Other things being equal, it's best to work in the business for which you have the best developed talent, but if you have a strong desire to engage in any particular line of work, you should choose that work as your ultimate goal. Although you'll get rich most easily if you do the things that fit you best, you'll get rich most satisfactorily if you do what you really want to do. Doing what you are drawn to do is Life, and there's no real satisfaction in living if we can never do what we want to do and are compelled forever to do something we don't enjoy.

Thankfully, you can indeed do what you want to do. The desire to do it is proof that you have the power to do it. Desire is a manifestation of power. Where there's no power, either developed or undeveloped, to do something, there's never any desire to do that thing. At the same time, *where there is a strong desire to do something, it's certain proof that the power to do it only requires to be developed and applied in the right way*. The desire to play music is the power to play music seeking expression and development through you. The desire to invent things is mechanical talent seeking expression and development.

If errors of judgment in the past have placed you in an undesirable business or environment today, you may have to do what you don't like to do for a while. You can make it easier by realizing that what you're doing now is making it possible for you to start doing what you really want to do in the future.

If you feel you're not in the right vocation, don't act too hastily in trying to get into another one. The best way, generally, to change our business or environment is by growth: as we said before, being more than the position requires until the environment shifts around us.

So never take sudden or radical action when you are in doubt as to the wisdom of doing so, but don't be afraid to make a sudden and radical change if the opportunity is presented and you feel, after careful consideration, that it's the right opportunity.

No Need to Hurry
There's never any hurry on the creative plane and no lack of op-

portunity. When you get out of the competitive mind, you'll understand that you never need to act hastily. No one else is going to beat you to the thing you want to do; there's plenty for all. If one space is taken, another, better one will open for you a little farther on; there's plenty of time. When you're in doubt, wait.[11] Fall back on the contemplation of your vision, and increase your faith and intention. And by all means, in times of doubt and indecision, cultivate gratitude.

There is a mind that knows all there is to know, and if you have deep gratitude, you can come into unity with this mind. As you go on acting in the way outlined in this book, opportunities will come to you in increasing number, and you'll need to be very steady in your faith and intention, keeping in close touch with the supreme mind with reverent gratitude, to make effective choices.

A day or two spent in contemplating the vision of what you want and in earnest thanksgiving that you are getting it will bring your mind into such close relationship with the Supreme that you'll make no mistake when you do act.

So, do all that you can do effectively every day, but do it without haste, worry, or fear. Move as quickly as you can, but never hurry. *Mistakes come from acting hastily, from acting in fear or doubt, or from forgetting the right motive, which is more life to all and less to none.*

Remember: the moment you begin to hurry you cease to be a creator and become a competitor, dropping back to the old plane again.

Whenever you find yourself hurrying, stop. Fix your attention on the mental image of the thing you want, and begin to give thanks that you are getting it. The exercise of

---

11 Michael Valentine Smith, in Robert Heinlein's *Stranger in a Strange Land*, demonstrates this, saying, "Waiting is."

gratitude will never fail to strengthen your faith and renew your intention.

SUMMARY

All other things being equal, it's best to choose the business for which you have the best developed talent, but if you have a strong desire for a particular line of work, you should set that work as your ultimate goal.

Don't be afraid to make a sudden and radical change if the opportunity is presented and you feel, after careful consideration, that it's the right opportunity. But never take sudden or radical action when you are in doubt as to the wisdom of doing so. Mistakes come from acting hastily, from acting in fear or doubt, or from forgetting the right motive, which is always more life to all and less to none.

No one else is going to beat you to the thing you want to do; there's plenty for all. If one space is taken, another and a better one will be opened for you a little farther on; there's plenty of time. When you're in doubt, wait.

A day or two spent in contemplating the vision of what you want and in earnest thanksgiving that you are getting it will bring your mind into such close relationship with the Supreme that you'll make no mistake when you do act.

14. THE IMPRESSION OF ENHANCEMENT

⚜

WHETHER YOU ultimately change your line of work or not, for the moment your actions must pertain to the business you're in now. You can get into the position you want by making constructive use of the position you're already in, doing your daily work in the specific way outlined here.

The Desire for Enhancement

To the extent that your work consists in dealing with other people, whether in person, by mail, by phone, or online, the main thought underlying all your actions must be to give them a sense of enhancement.

The desire for enhancement is inherent in all nature; it's the fundamental impulse of the universe. Every living thing needs continuous expansion and advance, and where increase of life ceases, dissolution and death set in at once.

Everyone instinctively knows this and, therefore, is forever seeking more: all human activities are based on the desire for enhancement. Everywhere people seek more food, nicer clothes, better shelter, more beauty, more knowledge, more pleasure; they all seek enhancement in some form, as an indication of more Life. And because it's the deepest instinct of their natures, all men and women are attracted to those who can give them more of the means of Life.

Jesus set forth the law of perpetual enhancement in the parable of the talents, which may be summarized as, "Only those who increase value retain any; from him who has not increased the value of what he has shall be taken away even what he has."

So, the normal desire for increased wealth is neither evil nor reprehensible; it's simply the desire for more abundant life. It's hope, aspiration. Enhancement is what all men and women seek; it's the urge of the formless intelligence within them seeking fuller expression.

By following the method described in this book, you're gaining continuously for yourself, and you're enhancing the life of all with whom you deal. *You are a creative center from which a sense of enhancement is radiating to all.*

Conveying the Impression

Be sure of this, and convey your assurance to every man, woman, and child with whom you come in contact. No matter how small the transaction, even if it's only selling a stick of candy to a child, put into it the idea of enhancement, and make sure that the customer catches the thought. Even to the people you meet socially, without any thought of business or selling anything, share the idea of enhancement.

In the process, you also convey the impression of advancement with everything you do, so everyone receives the impression that you are an advancing personality and that you will advance all who deal with you.

Do everything with the firm conviction that you are advancing yourself and enhancing the lives of everybody around you. Hold the unshakable faith that you are experiencing enhancement by letting this faith inspire, fill, and permeate every action. Feel that you are getting rich, and that, in so doing, you are making others rich, conferring the benefits on all.

But don't boast or brag of your success or talk about it unnecessarily; true faith is never boastful. Wherever you find a boastful person, you find someone who is secretly doubtful and afraid.

Simply feel the faith, and let it work out in every transaction. Let your every act and tone and look express the quiet assurance that you are getting rich—that you're already rich. Words won't be necessary to communicate this feeling to others.

You must so impress others with this idea that they feel that by associating with you they will experience enhancement for themselves. See that you give them a use value greater than any cash value you take from them. They'll feel the sense of enhancement in your presence, and they'll be attracted to you.

Take an honest pride in doing this, let everybody know it, and you will have no lack of customers. People go where they experience enhancement, and the Supreme, which desires enhancement in all and which knows all, will move toward you people who've never heard of you. Your business will increase rapidly, and you will be surprised at the unexpected benefits that will come to you. You'll be able each day to make better deals, secure greater advantages, and go on into a more congenial vocation if you desire to do so.

But in doing thing all this, you must never lose sight of your vision of what you want or your faith and intention to get what you want, with more for all in the process.

Enhancement of, Not Power Over

Let me here give you another word of caution in regard to motives: *Beware of the insidious temptation to seek power over other people.*

Nothing is so pleasant to the unformed or partially developed mind as the exercise of power over others. The desire to rule for selfish gratification has been the curse of the world. For countless ages governments and men have drenched the earth with blood in their battles to extend their dominions—not to seek more life for all, but to get more power for themselves.

Today, the main motive in the business and industrial world is often the same: men marshal their armies of dollars and lay waste the lives and hearts of millions in the mad scramble for power over others. Commercial kings, like political kings, are inspired by the lust for power.

Watch out for the temptation to seek for authority, to become a "master," to be considered above the common herd, to impress others by lavish display, and so on.

There's no need to rule over anyone in order to master your environment and your destiny. In fact, if you fall into the world's struggle for high places, you begin to be conquered by fate and circumstances and your becoming wealthy becomes subject to chance and speculation rather than the science described here. The mind that seeks mastery over others is the competitive mind, not the creative one.[12]

No better statement of the principle of creative action can be formulated than the favorite declaration of the late "Golden Rule" Jones of Toledo, Ohio: *"What I want for myself, I want for everybody."*[13]

---

12 Psychiatrist David Hawkins makes this distinction in *Power vs. Force*, saying that force is attempting to control others, while power is the capacity to accomplish.

13 Samuel M. Jones owned a factory in Toledo in the late 1800s and earned

SUMMARY

The main thought underlying all your interactions with others must be to give them a sense of enhancement. Do everything that you do with the firm conviction that you are an advancing personality and that you enhance the lives of all who deal with you. Feel that you are becoming wealthy, and that in doing so you are making others wealthy, conferring the benefits of your riches on all.

Impress others with this idea, so they feel that by associating with you their lives will be enhanced. See that you give them a use value greater than any cash value you take from them. Take an honest pride in doing this, let everybody know it, and you will have no lack of customers. People will go where they experience enhancement.

There's no need to rule over anyone in order to master your environment and your destiny. In fact, if you fall into that struggle, you begin to be conquered by fate and circumstances. The mind that seeks power over others is the competitive mind, not the creative one.

---

a reputation for honest business and fair dealings. He said his company needed only one policy—the Golden Rule, "Do unto others as you would have them do unto you"—and he nailed a plaque with that phrase to the factory wall. He did away with bosses and timekeepers, and his employees were among the first to receive vacations, paid holidays, insurance, and a park and playground. He became a popular mayor of Toledo, championing the public parks and publicly owned utilities. He replaced policemen's nightsticks with walking sticks and refused to prosecute so-called "morality laws," which he felt were unfair to the poor. In 1904, at the age of 57, Mr. Jones died suddenly while still in office. Not surprisingly, his funeral was said to be the largest and best attended in the city's history.

15. ADVANCEMENT

———————— ⚜ ————————

WHAT I said in the last chapter applies equally to the professional and the wage earner as it does to someone in sales or any other form of business.

Practicing Any Profession

No matter what profession you're in, whether you are a physician, a teacher, or a clergyman, if you can give increase of life to others and make them sensible of that fact, they will be attracted to you, they will support your work, and you will get rich.

The physician who holds the vision of himself as a great and successful healer, and who works toward the complete realization of that vision with faith and intention, as described in former chapters, will come into such close touch with the source of life that he will be phenomenally successful; patients will come to him in throngs.

No one has a greater opportunity to carry into effect this book's teaching than doctors, nurses, and other healing professionals. It doesn't matter which of the various forms of healing they may practice, for the principle of healing is common to all of them and may be reached by all alike. Healing professionals who hold a clear mental image of themselves as successful and who obey the laws of faith, intention, and gratitude will cure every curable case they undertake.

In the field of religion, the world cries out for clergy who can teach the true science of abundant life. The minister who masters the details of the science of getting rich, together with the allied sciences of being well, of being great, and of winning love, and who teaches these details from the pulpit will never lack for a congregation. This is a gospel that the world needs; it will enhance lives, and people will hear it gladly and give liberal support to the pastor who brings it to them.

We want preachers who cannot only tell us how, but who in their own lives will show us how. We need preachers who will themselves be rich, healthy, great, and beloved to teach us how to attain to these things, and they will find numerous and loyal followings.

The same is true of the teacher who can inspire children with the faith and intention of advancing life. Such a teacher will never be out of a job. And any teacher who has this faith and intention can give it to the students—can't help giving it to them if it's part of his or her own life and practice.

What is true of the teacher, preacher, and physician is true of the lawyer, dentist, engineer, or real estate or insurance agent—of everybody in every profession.

The combined mental and personal action I have described is infallible; it cannot fail. *Everyone who follows these instructions steadily, perseveringly, and to the letter will get rich.* The law of enhanced life is as mathematically

certain in its operation as the law of gravity. Getting rich is
an exact science.

Working for Wages

The wage earner will find this to be true, as well. Don't
feel you have no chance to get rich because you're working where there is no visible opportunity for advancement,
where wages are small and the cost of living high. Form
your clear mental vision of what you want, and begin to act
with faith and intention.

Do all the work you can do, every day, and do each piece
of work effectively. Put the power of success and the intention to get rich into everything that you do.

But don't do this merely with the idea of currying favor
with your employer, in the hope that those above you will
see your good work and advance you. It's not likely that they
will do so. People who are merely "good workers," filling
their places to the very best of their abilities and satisfied
with that, are valuable to their employers, and it's not in the
employer's interest to promote them. Such employees are
worth the most right where they are.

So don't try to more than fill your present position with
a view to pleasing your employer. Do it with the idea of advancing yourself.

The employees who advance are the ones who are too
big for their positions, who have a clear concept of what
they want to be, who know that they can become what they
want to be, and are determined to be that.

To get promoted, you have to do more than be effective
in your position. Hold the faith and intention of enhanced
life during work hours, after work hours, and before work
hours. Hold it in such a way that every person who comes in

contact with you feels the power of your intention radiating from you, and everyone gets the sense of advancement and increase from you. People will be attracted to you, and if there is no possibility for advancement in your present job, you will very soon see an opportunity to take another job.

There's nothing in your circumstances or in the economy that can keep you down. There's a power that never fails to present opportunities to the advancing personality who is moving in obedience to law. God can't help helping you if you act in the certain way we're describing here. The life force must do so in order to become more.

If you can't get rich working in industry, you can get rich on a ten-acre farm, or some other situation that suits your talents and desires. And if you begin to move in the certain way, you will certainly escape from the "clutches" of the corporation and get on to the farm or wherever else you wish to be.

Nobody has to work for a corporation. Big companies can keep people in so called "hopeless" conditions only as long as there are people who are ignorant of the science of getting rich or too intellectually lazy to practice it. If a few thousands of its employees would enter upon the certain way, the corporation would soon be in a bad plight. It would have to either give its workers more opportunity or go out of business.

Begin this way of thinking and acting, and your faith and intention will make you quick to see any opportunity to better your situation. Such opportunities will speedily come, for the supreme power, working in all and working for you, will bring them to you. There's no such thing in this universe as a lack of opportunities for the person who is living the advancing life.

So don't wait for "the ideal" opportunity to be all that you want to be. When an opportunity to be more than you are now is presented and you feel impelled toward it, take it. It's the first step toward an even greater opportunity.

If anyone thinks and acts according to the science described here, the constitution of the cosmos requires that all things shall be for him and work together for his good, and he must certainly get rich. So let wage earning men and women study this book with great care and enter with confidence upon the course of action it prescribes.

It will not fail.

SUMMARY

No matter what profession you're in, if you give increase of life to others and make them aware of that fact, they will be attracted to you, they will support your work, you will fulfill their needs, and you will get rich.

The wage earner will find this true, as well. Don't feel you have no chance to get rich because you're working where there's no visible opportunity for advancement, where wages are small, and the cost of living high.

To secure advancement, you have to do more than be effective in your position. Hold the faith and intention of increase during work hours, after work hours, and before work hours. Hold it in such a way that every person who comes in contact with you feels the power of intention radiating from you, and everyone gets a sense of advancement and increase from you. People will be attracted to you, and if there's no possibility for advancement in your present job, you will very soon see an opportunity to take another job.

There's nothing in your circumstances or in the economy that can keep you down.

Don't wait for "the ideal" opportunity to be all that you want to be. When an opportunity to be more than you are now is presented and you feel impelled toward it, take it. It's the first step toward an even greater opportunity.

16. SOME CAUTIONS AND CONCLUDING OBSERVATIONS

❧

Many people will scorn the idea that there's an exact science for getting rich. Believing that the supply of wealth is limited, they will insist that social and governmental institutions must be changed before any considerable number of people can accomplish it.

But this is not true.

Neither Government nor Economy Can Stop You

It is true that existing governments keep the masses in poverty, but this is because the masses don't think and act in the certain way we've outlined here. If the masses began to move forward as suggested in this book, neither governments nor industrial systems could hold them back. If the people have the advancing mind, have the faith that they can become rich, and move forward with the fixed intention to become rich, nothing can possibly keep them in poverty. All systems would be modified to accommodate the forward movement.

Anyone may enter upon the certain way at any time under any government and become rich. And when a significant number of people do so under any government, they open the way for others.[14]

The world's economic woes will only be solved when a large number of people practice the scientific method set down in this book and become rich. These will show others the way and inspire them with a desire for real Life, with the faith that it can be attained, and the intention to attain it. The more people who get rich on the competitive plane, the worse for others. The more who get rich on the creative plane, the better for everyone.

For now, it's enough to know that neither the government under which you live nor the capitalist or competitive system of industry can keep you from getting rich. When you enter the creative plane of thought, you will rise above all these things and become a citizen of another kingdom.

But remember that your thought *must* be held on the creative plane. You are never for an instant to regard the supply as limited or to act in competition.

Whenever you do fall into old ways of thought, correct yourself instantly. Simply cancel the old way of thought, and replace it with your declaration of gratitude for a limitless substance. Undo that old thought, for when you're in the competitive mind, you're "out of sync" with the cooperative supreme mind.

No Possible Future Event Is Worth Your Concern
Give no anxious thought to possible disasters, obstacles, panics, or unfavorable combinations of circumstances. There's

---

14 Perhaps the best documented illustration of this process is the reversal of apartheid in South Africa.

time enough to meet such situations when they present themselves. More, as you focus on the immediate present, you'll find that every difficulty carries with it the means to overcome it.

Don't spend any time planning how to meet possible emergencies in the future, except as those plans may affect your actions today. Your concern is with doing today's work in the most effective way, not with any emergencies that may arise tomorrow. You can attend to them as they come.

Don't be concerned about how to overcome possible emerging obstacles, unless you can see plainly that you must alter your course today to avoid them. No matter how huge an obstruction may appear at a distance, you'll find that, if you go on in the certain way, it will disappear as you approach it or that a way over, under, through, or around it will appear.

No possible combination of circumstances can defeat a man or woman who is proceeding to get rich along these strictly scientific lines. No one who obeys the law can fail to get rich any more than they could multiply two by two and fail to get four.

Speak Only From Faith and Intention

Guard your speech. Never speak of yourself, your affairs, or of anything else in a discouraged or discouraging way. Never admit the possibility of failure or speak in a way that infers failure as a possibility.

Never speak of the times as being hard or of business conditions as being doubtful. Times may be hard and business doubtful for those who are on the competitive plane, but they can never be so for you. *You can create what you want, so you're above fear.*

In what others consider hard times and poor business, you will find your greatest opportunities.

Train yourself to think of and see the world as something which is becoming, which is growing, and to regard seeming evil as only that which is undeveloped. Always speak in terms of advancement. To do otherwise is to deny your faith, and to deny your faith is to lose it.

No Need for Disappointment

Never allow yourself to feel disappointed. You may expect to have a certain thing at a certain time and not get it at that time, and this will appear to you like failure. But if you hold to your faith, you'll find that the failure is only apparent. As you go on in the certain way, if you don't receive that thing, you'll receive something so much better that the seeming failure becomes really a great success.

A student of this science had set his mind on making a certain business deal that seemed to be very desirable, and he worked for some weeks to bring it about. When the crucial time came, the thing failed in a perfectly inexplicable way. It was as if some unseen influence had been working secretly against him.

But he was not disappointed. On the contrary, he thanked God that his desire had been overruled and went steadily on with a grateful mind. In a few weeks, an opportunity came his way that was so much better he would never have considered the first deal, and he saw that a mind that knew more than he knew had prevented him from losing the greater good by entangling himself with the lesser.

That's the way every seeming failure will work out for you if you keep your faith, hold to your intention, have gratitude in all, and do, every day, all that can be done effectively that day.

When you experience what seems like failure, it's because you haven't asked for enough. Keep on, and something greater than you were seeking will certainly come to you.

Remember this.

All Skill and Wisdom Available

You will not fail because you lack the talent to do what you wish to do. Many people with little talent have succeeded greatly. If you go on as I've directed, you'll develop all the talent that is needed for your work.

It's not within the scope of this book to deal with the science of cultivating talent, but it's as certain and simple as the process of getting rich. However, don't hesitate for fear that when you come to any circumstance you might fail for lack of ability. Keep right on, and when you come to that place, the ability will be available to you. The same source of ability that enabled the untaught Abraham Lincoln to do the greatest work in government ever accomplished by a single man is open to you. You have access to all the mind there is for the wisdom to meet the responsibilities laid upon you. Go on in full faith.

Study this book. Make it your constant companion until you've mastered all the ideas contained in it. While you're getting firmly established in this faith, you'll do well to give up most recreations and to stay away from places where conflicting ideas are advanced in lectures or sermons. Don't read pessimistic or conflicting literature or get into arguments about it.

Spend most of your leisure time contemplating your vision, cultivating gratitude, and reading this book. It contains all you need to know of the science of getting rich, and you will find all the essentials summed up in the following chapter.

SUMMARY

Anyone can begin to follow the certain way at any time, under any government, and get rich.

Your concern is with doing today's work in the most effective way, not with any emergencies that may arise tomorrow. You can attend to them as they come.

Guard your speech. Never speak of yourself, your affairs, or of anything else in a discouraged or discouraging way.

You may expect to have a certain thing at a certain time and not get it at that time, and this will appear to you like failure. But as you go on in the certain way, if you don't receive that thing, you'll receive something so much better that the seeming failure becomes a great success.

Don't hesitate for fear that you will fail for lack of ability. Keep right on, and when you come to the place you need it, the ability will be furnished to you.

17 . A SUMMARY OF THE SCIENCE OF GETTING RICH

———— ⚜ ————

THERE IS a thinking stuff from which all things are made and which, in its original state, permeates, penetrates, and fills the interspaces of the universe.

A thought in this substance produces the thing that is imaged in the thought.

Human beings can form things in our thoughts and, by impressing our thoughts upon the formless substance, can cause the thing we think about to be created.

In order to do this, we must pass from the competitive mind to the creative mind, otherwise we aren't in harmony with formless intelligence, which is always creative and never competitive in spirit.

Anyone may come into full harmony with the formless substance by entertaining a lively and sincere gratitude for the blessings it bestows upon us. Gratitude unifies the minds of individuals with the intelligence of substance, so that our thoughts are received by the formless.

We can stay on the creative plane only by uniting ourselves with the formless intelligence through a deep and continuous feeling of gratitude.

We must form a clear and definite mental image of the things we wish to have, to do, or to become, and we must hold this mental image in our thoughts, while being deeply grateful to the Supreme that all our desires are granted to us. If we wish to get rich, we must use our leisure hours contemplating our vision, in earnest thanksgiving that the reality is being given to us.

The importance of frequent contemplation of the mental image, coupled with unwavering faith and devout gratitude can't be over-emphasized. This is the process by which the impression is given to the formless and creative forces are set in motion.

Creative energy works through established channels of natural growth and the economic and social order. All that is included in their mental image will surely be brought to anyone who follows the instructions given above and whose faith does not waver. What we desire will come to us through the ways of established trade and commerce.

In order to receive our own when it's ready to come to us, we must be acting in a way that causes us to more than fill our present position. We must keep in mind our intention to get rich through realization of our mental image. And we must do, every day, all that can be done that day, taking care to do each thing effectively. We must give to every person a use value greater than the cash value we receive, so that each transaction increases life, and we must be so firm in our conviction of increase that the impression will be communicated to all with whom we comes into contact.

The men and women who practice the foregoing instructions will certainly get rich, and the riches they receive will be in exact proportion to the clarity of their vision, the firmness of their intention, the steadiness of their faith, and the depth of their gratitude.

ORIGINAL TEXT

I. THE RIGHT TO BE RICH

⚜

WHATEVER MAY be said in praise of poverty, the fact remains that it is not possible to live a really complete or successful life unless one is rich. No man can rise to his greatest possible height in talent or soul development unless he has plenty of money; for to unfold the soul and to develop talent, he must have many things to use, and he cannot have these things unless he has money to buy them with.

A man develops in mind, soul, and body by making use of things, and society is so organized that man must have money in order to become the possessor of things; therefore, the basis of all advancement for man must be The Science of Getting Rich.

The object of all life is development; and everything that lives has an inalienable right to all the development it is capable of attaining.

Man's right to life means his right to have the free and unrestricted use of all the things which may be necessary to his fullest mental, spiritual, and physical unfoldment or, in other words, his right to be rich.

In this book, I shall not speak of riches in a figurative way; to be really rich does not mean to be satisfied or contented with a little. No man ought to be satisfied with a little if he is capable of using and enjoying more. The purpose of Nature is the advancement and unfoldment of life, and every man should have all that can contribute to the power, elegance, beauty, and richness of life; to be content with less is sinful.

The man who owns all he wants for the living of all the life he is capable of living is rich; and no man who has not plenty of money can have all he wants. Life has advanced so far and become so complex, that even the most ordinary man or woman requires a great amount of wealth in order to live in a manner that even approaches completeness. Every person naturally wants to become all that they are capable of becoming; this desire to realize innate possibilities is inherent in human nature; we cannot help wanting to be all that we can be. Success in life is becoming what you want to be; you can become what you want to be only by making use of things, and you can have the free use of things only as you become rich enough to buy them. To understand The Science of Getting Rich is therefore the most essential of all knowledge.

There is nothing wrong in wanting to get rich. The desire for riches is really the desire for a richer, fuller, and more abundant life; and that desire is praiseworthy. The man who does not desire to live more abundantly is abnormal, and so the man who does not desire to have money enough to buy all he wants is abnormal.

There are three motives for which we live: we live for the body, we live for the mind, we live for the soul. No one of these is better or holier than the other; all are alike desirable, and no one of the three—body, mind, or soul—can live fully if either of the others is cut short of full life and expression. It is not right or noble to live only for the soul and deny mind or body; and it is wrong to live for the intellect and deny body or soul.

We are all acquainted with the loathsome consequences of living for the body and denying both mind and soul; and we see that *real* life means the complete expression of all that man can give forth through body, mind, and soul. Whatever he can say, no man can be really happy or satisfied unless his body is living fully in every function and unless the same is true of his mind and his soul. Wherever there is unexpressed possibility, or function not performed, there is unsatisfied desire. Desire is possibility seeking expression, or function seeking performance.

Man cannot live fully in body without good food, comfortable clothing, warm shelter, and without freedom from excessive toil. Rest and recreation are also necessary to his physical life.

He cannot live fully in mind without books and time to study them, without opportunity for travel and observation, or without intellectual companionship.

To live fully in mind, he must have intellectual recreations and must surround himself with all the objects of art and beauty he is capable of using and appreciating.

To live fully in soul, man must have love; and love is denied expression by poverty.

A man's highest happiness is found in the bestowal of benefits on those he loves; love finds its most natural and spontaneous expression in giving. The man who has nothing to give cannot fill his place as a husband or father, as a citizen, or as a man. It is in the use of material things that a man finds full life for his body, develops his mind, and unfolds his soul. It is therefore of supreme importance to him that he should be rich.

It is perfectly right that you should desire to be rich; if you are a normal man or woman, you cannot help doing so. It is perfectly right that you should give your best attention to The Science of Getting Rich, for it is the noblest and most necessary of all studies. If you neglect this study, you are derelict in your duty to yourself, to God, and to humanity; for you can render to God and humanity no greater service than to make the most of yourself.

2. THERE IS A SCIENCE OF GETTING RICH

———— ❧ ————

THERE IS a Science of Getting Rich, and it is an exact science, like algebra or arithmetic. There are certain laws which govern the process of acquiring riches; once these laws are learned and obeyed by any man, he will get rich with mathematical certainty.

The ownership of money and property comes as a result of doing things in a Certain Way; those who do things in this Certain Way, whether on purpose or accidentally, get rich; while those who do not do things in this Certain Way, no matter how hard they work or how able they are, remain poor.

It is a natural law that like causes always produce like effects; therefore, any man or woman who learns to do things in this certain way will infallibly get rich.

That the above statement is true is shown by the following facts.

Getting rich is not a matter of environment, for, if it were, all the people in certain neighborhoods would become wealthy; the people of one city would all be rich, while those of other towns would all be poor; or the inhabitants of one state would roll in wealth, while those of an adjoining state would be in poverty.

But everywhere we see rich and poor living side by side in the same environment and often engaged in the same vocations. When two men are in the same locality, and in the same business, and one gets rich while the other remains poor, it shows that getting rich is not, primarily, a matter of environment. Some environments may be more favorable than others, but when two men in the same business are in the same neighborhood, and one gets rich while the other fails, it indicates that getting rich is the result of doing things in a Certain Way.

And further, the ability to do things in this Certain Way is not due solely to the possession of talent, for many people who have great talent remain poor, while others who have very little talent get rich.

Studying the people who have become rich, we find that they are an average lot in all respects, having no greater talents and abilities than other men. It is evident that they do not get rich because they possess talents and abilities that other men have not, but because they happen to do things in a Certain Way.

Getting rich is not the result of saving, or "thrift"; many very penurious people are poor, while free spenders often get rich.

Nor is getting rich due to doing things which others fail to do; for two men in the same business often do almost exactly the same things, and one gets rich while the other remains poor or becomes bankrupt.

From all these things, we must come to the conclusion that getting rich is the result of doing things in a Certain Way.

If getting rich is the result of doing things in a Certain Way, and if like causes always produce like effects, then any man or woman who can do things in that Way can become rich, and the whole matter is brought within the domain of exact science.

The question arises here whether this Certain Way may not be so difficult that only a few may follow it. This cannot be true, as we have seen, so far as natural ability is concerned. Talented people get rich, and blockheads get rich; intellectually brilliant people get rich, and very stupid people get rich; physically strong people get rich, and weak and sickly people get rich.

Some degree of ability to think and understand is, of course, essential; but insofar as natural ability is concerned, any man or woman who has sense enough to read and understand these words can certainly get rich.

Also, we have seen that it is not a matter of environment. Location counts for something; one would not go to the heart of the Sahara and expect to do successful business. Getting rich involves the necessity of dealing with men and of being where there are people to deal with; and if these people are inclined to deal in the way you want to deal, so much the better. But that is about as far as environment goes.

If anybody else in your town can get rich, so can you; and if anybody else in your state can get rich, so can you.

Again, it is not a matter of choosing some particular business or profession. People get rich in every business and in every profession; while their next door neighbors in the same vocation remain in poverty.

It is true that you will do best in a business which you like and which is congenial to you; and if you have certain talents which are well developed, you will do best in a business which calls for the exercise of those talents.

Also, you will do best in a business which is suited to your locality; an ice-cream parlor would do better in a warm climate than in Greenland, and a salmon fishery will succeed better in the Northwest than in Florida, where there are no salmon.

But, aside from these general limitations, getting rich is not dependent upon your engaging in some particular business, but upon your learning to do things in a Certain Way. If you are now in business, and anybody else in your locality is getting rich in the same business while you are not getting rich, it is because you are not doing things in the same Way that the other person is doing them.

No one is prevented from getting rich by lack of capital. True, as you get capital the increase becomes easier and quicker; but one who has capital is already rich and does not need to consider how to become so. No matter how poor you may be, if you begin to do things in the Certain Way, you will begin to get rich; and you will begin to have capital. The getting of capital is a part of the process of getting rich; and it is a part of the result which invariably follows the doing of things in the Certain Way. You may be the poorest man on the continent and be deeply in debt; you may have neither friends, influence, nor resources; but if you begin to do things in this way, you must infallibly begin to get rich, for like causes must produce like effects. If you have no capital, you can get capital; if you are in the wrong business, you can get into the right business; if you are in the wrong location, you can go to the right location; and you can do so *by beginning in your present business and in your present location* to do things in the Certain Way which causes success.

3. IS OPPORTUNITY MONOPOLIZED?

⚜

NO MAN is kept poor because opportunity has been taken away from him or because other people have monopolized the wealth and have put a fence around it. You may be shut off from engaging in business in certain lines, but there are other channels open to you. Probably it would be hard for you to get control of any of the great railroad systems; that field is pretty well monopolized. But the electric railway business is still in its infancy and offers plenty of scope for enterprise; and it will be but a very few years until traffic and transportation through the air will become a great industry and, in all its branches, will give employment to hundreds of thousands, and perhaps to millions, of people. Why not turn your attention to the development of aerial transportation, instead of competing with J. J. Hill and others for a chance in the steam railway world?

It is quite true that if you are a workman in the employ of the steel trust, you have very little chance of becoming the owner of the plant in which you work; but it is also true that if you will commence to act in a Certain Way, you can soon leave the employ of the steel trust; you can buy a farm of from ten to forty acres and engage in business as a producer of foodstuffs. There is great opportunity at this time for men who will live upon small tracts of land and cultivate the same intensively; such men will certainly get rich. You may say that it is impossible for you to get the land, but I am going to prove to you that it is not impossible and that you can certainly get a farm if you will go to work in a Certain Way.

At different periods, the tide of opportunity sets in different directions, according to the needs of the whole and the particular stage of social evolution which has been reached. At present, in America, it is setting toward agriculture and the allied industries and professions. Today, opportunity is open before the factory worker in his line. It is open before the businessman who supplies the farmer more than before the one who supplies the factory worker; and before the professional man who waits upon the farmer more than before the one who serves the working class.

There is abundance of opportunity for the man who will go with the tide, instead of trying to swim against it.

So the factory workers, either as individuals or as a class, are not deprived of opportunity. The workers are not being "kept down" by their masters; they are not being "ground" by the trusts and combinations of capital. As a class, they are where they are because they do not do things in a Certain Way. If the workers of America chose to do so, they could follow the example of their brothers in Belgium and other countries and establish great department stores and co-operative industries; they could elect men of their own class to office and pass laws favoring the development of such co-operative industries; and in a few years they could take peaceable possession of the industrial field.

The working class may become the master class if they will begin to do things in a Certain Way; the law of wealth is the same for them as it is for all others. This they must learn, and they will remain where they are as long as they continue to do as they do. The individual worker, however, is not held down by the ignorance or the mental slothfulness of his class; he can follow the tide of opportunity to riches, and this book will tell him how.

No one is kept in poverty by a shortness in the supply of riches; there is more than enough for all. A palace as large as the capitol at Washington might be built for every family on earth from the building material in the United States alone; and under intensive cultivation, this country would produce wool, cotton, linen, and silk enough to clothe each person in the world finer than Solomon was arrayed in all his glory; all this together with food enough to feed them all luxuriously.

The visible supply is practically inexhaustible, and the invisible supply really is inexhaustible.

Everything you see on earth is made from one original substance, out of which all things proceed.

New Forms are constantly being made, and older ones are dissolving; but all are shapes assumed by One Thing.

There is no limit to the supply of Formless Stuff, or Original Substance. The universe is made out of it, but it was not all used in making the universe. The spaces in, through, and between the forms of the visible universe are permeated and filled with the Original Substance, with the Formless Stuff, with the raw material of all things. Ten thousand times as much as has been made might still be made, and even then we should not have exhausted the supply of universal raw material.

No man, therefore, is poor because nature is poor or because there is not enough to go around.

Nature is an inexhaustible storehouse of riches; the supply will never run short. Original Substance is alive with creative energy and is constantly producing more forms. When the supply of building material is exhausted, more will be produced; when the soil is exhausted so that foodstuffs and materials for clothing will no longer grow upon it, it will be renewed or more soil will be made. When all the gold and silver has been dug from the earth, if man is still in such a stage of social development that he needs gold and silver, more will be produced from the Formless. The Formless Stuff responds to the needs of man; it will not let him be without any good thing.

This is true of man collectively; the race as a whole is always abundantly rich, and if individuals are poor, it is because they do not follow the Certain Way of doing things which makes the individual man rich.

The Formless Stuff is intelligent; it is stuff which thinks. It is alive and is always impelled toward more life.

It is the natural and inherent impulse of life to seek to live more; it is the nature of intelligence to enlarge itself and of consciousness to seek to extend its boundaries and find fuller expression. The universe of forms has been made by Formless Living Substance, throwing itself into form in order to express itself more fully.

The universe is a great Living Presence, always moving inherently toward more life and fuller functioning.

Nature is formed for the advancement of life; its impelling motive is the increase of life. For this cause, everything which can possibly minister to life is bountifully provided; there can be no lack unless God is to contradict himself and nullify his own works.

You are not kept poor by lack in the supply of riches; it is a fact which I shall demonstrate a little farther on that even the resources of the Formless Supply are at the command of the man or woman who will act and think in a Certain Way.

4. THE FIRST PRINCIPLE IN THE SCIENCE OF GETTING RICH

—————— ⚜ ——————

THOUGHT IS the only power which can produce tangible riches from the Formless Substance. The stuff from which all things are made is a substance which thinks, and a thought of form in this substance produces the form.

Original Substance moves according to its thoughts; every form and process you see in nature is the visible expression of a thought in Original Substance. As the Formless Stuff thinks of a form, it takes that form; as it thinks of a motion, it makes that motion. That is the way all things were created. We live in a thought world, which is part of a thought universe. The thought of a moving universe extended throughout Formless Substance, and the Thinking Stuff moving according to that thought, took the form of systems of planets and maintains that form. Thinking Substance takes the form of its thought and moves according to the thought. Holding the idea of a circling system of suns and worlds, it takes the form of these bodies and moves them as it thinks. Thinking the form of a slow-growing oak tree, it moves accordingly and produces the tree, though centuries may be required to do the work. In creating, the Formless seems to move according to the lines of motion it has established; the thought of an oak tree does not cause the instant formation of a full-grown tree, but it does start in motion the forces which will produce the tree, along established lines of growth.

Every thought of form, held in thinking Substance, causes the creation of the form, but always, or at least generally, along lines of growth and action already established.

The thought of a house of a certain construction, if it were impressed upon Formless Substance, might not cause the instant formation of the house, but it would cause the turning of creative energies already working in trade and commerce into such channels as to result in the speedy building of the house. And if there were no existing channels through which the creative energy could work, then the house would be formed directly from primal substance, without waiting for the slow processes of the organic and inorganic world.

No thought of form can be impressed upon Original Substance without causing the creation of the form.

Man is a thinking center and can originate thought. All the forms that man fashions with his hands must first exist in his thought; he cannot shape a thing until he has thought that thing. And so far, man has confined his efforts wholly to the work of his hands; he has applied manual labor to the world of forms, seeking to change or modify those already existing. He has never thought of trying to cause the creation of new forms by impressing his thoughts upon Formless Substance.

When man has a thought form, he takes material from the forms of nature and makes an image of the form which is in his mind. He has, so far, made little or no effort to co-operate with Formless Intelligence, to work "with the Father." He has not dreamed that he can "do what he seeth the Father doing." Man reshapes and modifies existing forms by manual labor; he has given no attention to the question of whether he may produce things from Formless Substance by communicating his thoughts to it. We propose to prove that he may do so, to prove that any man or woman may do so, and to show how. As our first step, we must lay down three fundamental propositions.

First, we assert that there is one Original Formless Stuff, or substance, from which all things are made. All the seemingly many elements are but different presentations of one element; all the many forms found in organic and inorganic nature are but different shapes made from the same stuff. And this stuff is Thinking Stuff; a thought held in it produces the form of the thought. Thought, in thinking substance, produces shapes. Man is a thinking center, capable of original thought; if man can communicate his thought to Original Thinking Substance, he can cause the creation, or formation, of the thing he thinks about. To summarize this:

There is a Thinking Stuff from which all things are made and which, in its original state, permeates, penetrates, and fills the interspaces of the universe.

A thought, in this substance, produces the thing that is imaged by the thought.

Man can form things in his thought and, by impressing his thought upon Formless Substance, can cause the thing he thinks about to be created.

It may be asked if I can prove these statements, and without going into details, I answer that I can do so, both by logic and experience.

Reasoning back from the phenomena of form and thought, I come to one Original Thinking Substance; and reasoning forward from this thinking substance, I come to man's power to cause the formation of the thing he thinks about.

And by experiment, I find the reasoning true, and this is my strongest proof.

If one man who reads this book gets rich by doing what it tells him to do, that is evidence in support of my claim; but if every man who does what it tells him to do gets rich, that is positive proof until someone goes through the process and fails. The theory is true until the process fails; and this process will not fail, for every man who does exactly what this book tells him to do will get rich.

I have said that men get rich by doing things in a Certain Way, and in order to do so, men must become able to think in a Certain Way.

A man's way of doing things is the direct result of the way he thinks about things.

To do things in a way you want to do them, you will have to acquire the ability to think the way you want to think; this is the first step toward getting rich.

To think what you want to think is to think truth, *regardless of appearances.*

Every man has the natural and inherent power to think what he wants to think, but it requires far more effort to do so than it does to think the thoughts which are suggested by appearances. To think according to appearance is easy; to think truth regardless of appearances is laborious and requires the expenditure of more power than any other work man is called upon to perform.

There is no labor from which most people shrink as they do from that of sustained and consecutive thought; it is the hardest work in the world. This is especially true when truth is contrary to appearances. Every appearance in the visible world tends to produce a corresponding form in the mind which observes it; and this can only be prevented by holding the thought of the *truth*.

To look upon the appearance of disease will produce the form of disease in your own mind, and ultimately in your body, unless you hold the thought of the truth, which is that there is no disease; it is only an appearance, and the reality is health.

To look upon the appearances of poverty will produce corresponding forms in your own mind, unless you hold to the truth that there is no poverty; there is only abundance.

To think health when surrounded by the appearances of disease, or to think riches when in the midst of appearances of poverty, requires power; but he who acquires this power becomes a *mastermind*. He can conquer fate; he can have what he wants.

This power can only be acquired by getting hold of the basic fact which is behind all appearances; that fact is that there is one Thinking Substance, from which and by which all things are made.

Then we must grasp the truth that every thought held in this substance becomes a form and that man can so impress his thoughts upon it as to cause them to take form and become visible things.

When we realize this, we lose all doubt and fear, for we know that we can create what we want to create; we can get what we want to have, and we can become what we want to be. As a first step toward getting rich, you must believe the three fundamental statements given previously in this chapter and, in order to emphasize them, I repeat them here:

There is a Thinking Stuff from which all things are made and which, in its original state, permeates, penetrates, and fills the interspaces of the universe.

A thought, in this substance, produces the thing that is imaged by the thought.

Man can form things in his thought and, by impressing his thought upon Formless Substance, can cause the thing he thinks about to be created.

You must lay aside all other concepts of the universe than this monistic one; and you must dwell upon this until it is fixed in your mind and has become your habitual thought. Read these creed statements over and over again; fix every word upon your memory, and meditate upon them until you firmly believe what they say. If a doubt comes to you, cast it aside as a sin. Do not listen to arguments against this idea; do not go to churches or lectures where a contrary concept of things is taught or preached. Do not read magazines or books which teach a different idea; if you get mixed up in your faith, all your efforts will be in vain.

Do not ask why these things are true, nor speculate as to how they can be true; simply take them on trust. The Science of Getting Rich begins with the absolute acceptance of this faith.

5. INCREASING LIFE

———————— ⚜ ————————

YOU MUST get rid of the last vestige of the old idea that there is a deity whose will it is that you should be poor or whose purposes may be served by keeping you in poverty.

The Intelligent Substance which is All, and in All, and which lives in All and lives in you, is a consciously Living Substance. Being a consciously Living Substance, It must have the nature and inherent desire of every living intelligence for increase of life. Every living thing must continually seek for the enlargement of its life because life, in the mere act of living, must increase itself.

A seed, dropped into the ground, springs into activity and, in the act of living, produces a hundred more seeds; life, by living, multiplies itself. It is forever becoming more; it must do so if it continues to be at all.

Intelligence is under this same necessity for continuous increase. Every thought we think makes it necessary for us to think another thought; consciousness is continually expanding. Every fact we learn leads us to the learning of another fact; knowledge is continually increasing. Every talent we cultivate brings to the mind the desire to cultivate another talent; we are subject to the urge of life seeking expression, which ever drives us on to know more, to do more, and to be more.

In order to know more, do more, and be more, we must have more; we must have things to use, for we learn, do, and become only by using things. We must get rich, so that we can live more.

The desire for riches is simply the capacity for larger life seeking fulfillment; every desire is the effort of an unexpressed possibility to come into action. It is power seeking to manifest which causes desire. That which makes you want more money is the same as that which makes the plant grow; it is Life seeking fuller expression.

The One Living Substance must be subject to this inherent law of all life; it is permeated with the desire to live more, which is why it is under the necessity of creating things.

The One Substance desires to live more in you; hence, it wants you to have all the things you can use.

It is the desire of God that you should get rich. He wants you to get rich because He can express Himself better through you if you have plenty of things to use in giving Him expression. He can live more in you if you have unlimited command of the means of life.

The universe desires you to have everything you want to have.

Nature is friendly to your plans.

Everything is naturally for you.

Make up your mind that this is true.

It is essential, however, that *your purpose should harmonize with the purpose that is in All.*

You must want real life, not mere pleasure of sensual gratification. Life is the performance of function; and the

individual really lives only when he performs every function—physical, mental, and spiritual—of which he is capable, without excess in any.

You do not want to get rich in order to live swinishly,
for the gratification of animal desires; that is not life. But
the performance of every physical function is a part of life,
and no one lives completely who denies the impulses of the
body, a normal and healthful expression.

You do not want to get rich solely to enjoy mental pleasures, to get knowledge, to gratify ambition, to outshine
others, to be famous. All these are legitimate parts of life,
but the man who lives for the pleasures of the intellect alone
will only have a partial life, and he will never be satisfied
with his lot.

You do not want to get rich solely for the good of others, to
lose yourself for the salvation of mankind, to experience the joys of
philanthropy and sacrifice. The joys of the soul are only a part of
life; and they are no better or nobler than any other part.

You want to get rich in order that you may eat, drink,
and be merry when it is time to do these things; in order that
you may surround yourself with beautiful things, see distant
lands, feed your mind, and develop your intellect; in order
that you may love men and do kind things, and be able to play
a good part in helping the world to find truth.

But remember that extreme altruism is no better and no
nobler than extreme selfishness; both are mistakes.

Get rid of the idea that God wants you to sacrifice yourself for others, and that you can secure His favor by doing
so; God requires nothing of the kind.

What He wants is that you should make the most of
yourself, for yourself, and for others, and *you can help others
more by making the most of yourself than in any other way.*

You can make the most of yourself only by getting rich, so it is right and praiseworthy that you should give your first and best thought to the work of acquiring wealth.

Remember, however, that the desire of Substance is for all, and its movements must be for more life to all; it cannot be made to work for less life to any because it is equally in all who are seeking riches and life.

Intelligent Substance will make things for you, but it will not take things away from someone else and give them to you.

You must get rid of the thought of competition. You are to create, not to compete for what is already created.

You do not have to take anything away from anyone.

You do not have to drive sharp bargains.

You do not have to cheat or take advantage. You do not need to let any man work for you for less than he earns.

You do not have to covet the property of others or look at it with wishful eyes; no man has anything of which you cannot have the like, and that without taking what he has away from him.

You are to become a creator, not a competitor; you are going to get what you want, but in such a way that, when you get it, every other man will have more than he has now.

I am aware that there are men who get a vast amount of money by proceeding in direct opposition to the statements in the paragraph above and should add a word of explanation here. Men of the plutocratic type, who become very rich, do so sometimes purely by their extraordinary ability on the plane of competition; sometimes they unconsciously relate themselves to Substance in its great purposes and movements for the general racial upbuilding through industrial evolution. Rockefeller, Carnegie, Morgan, et al., have been the unconscious agents of the Supreme in the necessary work of systematizing and organizing productive industry. In the end, their work will contribute immensely toward increased life for all. Their day is nearly over; they have organized production and *will soon be succeeded by the agents of the multitude, who will organize the machinery of distribution.*

The multimillionaires are like the monster reptiles of the prehistoric eras; they play a necessary part in the evolutionary process, but the same Power which produced them will dispose of them. And it is well to bear in mind that they have never been really rich; a record of the private lives of most of this class will show that they have really been the most abject and wretched of the poor.

Riches secured on the competitive plane are never satisfactory and permanent; they are yours today and another's tomorrow. Remember, if you are to become rich in a scientific and certain way, you must rise entirely out of the competitive thought. You must never think for a moment that the supply is limited. Just as soon as you begin to think that all the money is being "cornered" and controlled by bankers and others, and that you must exert yourself to get laws passed to stop this process, in that moment, you drop into the competitive mind, and your power to cause creation is gone for the time being. What is worse, you will probably arrest the creative movements you have already instituted.

Know that there are countless millions of dollars' worth of gold in the mountains of the earth, not yet brought to light; and know that if there were not, more would be created from Thinking Substance to supply your needs.

Know that the money you need will come, even if it is necessary for a thousand men to be led to the discovery of new gold mines tomorrow.

Never look at the visible supply; look always at the limitless riches in Formless Substance, and know *that they are coming to you as fast as you can receive and use them.* Nobody, by cornering the visible supply, can prevent you from getting what is yours.

So never allow yourself to think for an instant that all the best building spots will be taken before you get ready to build your house unless you hurry. Never worry about the trusts and combines and get anxious for fear they will soon come to own the whole earth. Never get afraid that you will lose what you want because some other person "beats you to it." That cannot possibly happen; you are not seeking any thing that is possessed by anybody else; you are causing what you want to be created from Formless Substance, and the supply is without limits. Stick to the formulated statement:

There is a Thinking Stuff from which all things are made and which, in its original state, permeates, penetrates, and fills the interspaces of the universe.

A thought, in this substance, produces the thing that is imaged by the thought.

Man can form things in his thought and, by impressing his thought upon Formless Substance, can cause the thing he thinks about to be created.

6. HOW RICHES COME TO YOU

❧

WHEN I say that you do not have to drive sharp bargains, I do not mean that you do not have to drive any bargains at all or that you are above the necessity for having any dealings with your fellow men. I mean that you will not need to deal with them unfairly; you do not have to get something for nothing *but can give to every man more than you take from him.*

You cannot give every man more in cash market value than you take from him, but you can give him more in use value than the cash value of the thing you take from him. The paper, ink, and other material in this book may not be worth the money you pay for it; but if the ideas suggested by it bring you thousands of dollars, you have not been wronged by those who sold it to you; they have given you a great use value for a small cash value.

Let us suppose that I own a picture by one of the great artists, which, in any civilized community, is worth thousands of dollars. I take it to Baffin Ray and, by "salesmanship," induce an Eskimo to give a bundle of furs worth $500 for it. I have really wronged him, for he has no use for the picture;

it has no use value to him; it will not add to his life.

But suppose I give him a gun worth $50 for his furs; then he has made a good bargain. He has use for the gun; it will get him many more furs and much food; it will add to his life in every way; it will make him rich.

When you rise from the competitive to the creative plane, you can scan your business transactions very strictly, and if you are selling any man anything which does not add more to his life than the thing he gives you in exchange, you can afford to stop it. You do not have to beat anybody in business. And if you are in a business which does beat people, get out of it at once.

Give every man more in use value than you take from him in cash value; then you are adding to the life of the world by every business transaction.

If you have people working for you, you must take from them more in cash value than you pay them in wages; but you can so organize your business that it will be filled with the principle of advancement and so that each employee who wishes to do so may advance a little every day.

You can make your business do for your employees what this book is doing for you. You can so conduct your business that it will be a sort of ladder, by which every employee who will take the trouble may climb to riches himself; and if given the opportunity he will not do so, it is not your fault.

And finally, because you are to cause the creation of your riches from Formless Substance which permeates all your environment, it does not follow that they are to take shape from the atmosphere and come into being before your eyes.

If you want a sewing machine, for instance, I do not mean to tell you that you are to impress the thought of a sewing machine on Thinking Substance until the machine is formed without hands, in the room where you sit or elsewhere. But if you want a sewing machine, hold the mental image of it with the most positive certainty that it is being made or is on its way to you. After once forming the thought, have the most absolute and unquestioning faith that the sewing machine is coming; never think of it or speak of it in any other way than as being sure to arrive. Claim it as already yours.

It will be brought to you by the power of the Supreme Intelligence, acting upon the minds of men. If you live in Maine, it may be that a man will be brought from Texas or Japan to engage in some transaction which will result in your getting what you want.

If so, the whole matter will be as much to that man's advantage as it is to yours.

Do not forget for a moment that the Thinking Substance is through all, in all, communicating with all, and can influence all. The desire of Thinking Substance for fuller life and better living has caused the creation of all the sewing machines already made; and it can cause the creation of millions more and will, whenever men set it in motion by desire and faith and by acting in a Certain Way.

You can certainly have a sewing machine in your house; and it is just as certain that you can have any other thing or things which you want and which you will use for the advancement of your own life and the lives of others.

You need not hesitate about asking largely; "it is your Father's pleasure to give you the kingdom," said Jesus.

Original Substance wants to live all that is possible in you and wants you to have all that you can or will use for the living of the most abundant life.

If you fix upon your consciousness the fact that the desire you feel for the possession of riches is one with the desire of Omnipotence for more complete expression, your faith becomes invincible.

Once I saw a little boy sitting at a piano and vainly trying to bring harmony out of the keys; and I saw that he was grieved and provoked by his inability to play real music. I asked him the cause of his vexation, and he answered, "I can feel the music in me, but I can't make my hands go right." The music in him was the *urge* of Original Substance, containing all the possibilities of all life; all that there is of music was seeking expression through the child.

God, the One Substance, is trying to live and do and enjoy things through humanity. He is saying "I want hands to build wonderful structures, to play divine harmonies, to paint glorious pictures; I want feet to run my errands, eyes to see my beauties, tongues to tell mighty truths and to sing marvelous songs," and so on.

All that there is of possibility is seeking expression through men. God wants those who can play music to have pianos and every other instrument and to have the means to cultivate their talents to the fullest extent; He wants those who can appreciate beauty to be able to surround themselves with beautiful things; He wants those who can discern truth to have every opportunity to travel and observe; He wants those who can appreciate dress to be beautifully clothed and those who can appreciate good food to be luxuriously fed.

He wants all these things because it is Himself that enjoys and appreciates them; it is God who wants to play, and sing, and enjoy beauty, and proclaim truth, and wear fine clothes, and eat good foods. "It is God that worketh in you to will and to do," said Paul.

The desire you feel for riches is the infinite seeking to express Himself in you as He sought to find expression in the little boy at the piano.

So you need not hesitate to ask largely.

Your part is to focalize and express the desire to God.

This is a difficult point with most people; they retain something of the old idea that poverty and self-sacrifice are pleasing to God. They look upon poverty as a part of the plan, a necessity of nature. They have the idea that God has finished His work and made all that He can make, and that the majority of men must stay poor because there is not enough to go around. They hold to so much of this erroneous thought that they feel ashamed to ask for wealth; they try not to want more than a very modest competence, just enough to make them fairly comfortable.

I recall now the case of one student who was told that he must get in mind a clear picture of the things he desired, so that the creative thought of them might be impressed on Formless Substance. He was a very poor man, living in a rented house and having only what he earned from day to day; and he could not grasp the fact that all wealth was his. So, after thinking the matter over, he decided that he might reasonably ask for a new rug for the floor of his best room and an anthracite coal stove to heat the house during the cold weather. Following the instructions given in this book, he obtained these things in a few months; and then it dawned upon him that he had not asked enough. He went through the house in which he lived and planned all the improvements he would like to make in it; he mentally added a bay window here and a room there, until it was complete in his mind as his ideal home; and then he planned its furnishings.

Holding the whole picture in his mind, he began living in the Certain Way and moving toward what he wanted; and he owns the house now and is rebuilding it after the form of his mental image. And now, with still larger faith, he is going on to get greater things. It has been unto him according to his faith, and it is so with you and with all of us.

7 . GRATITUDE

――――――― ⚜ ―――――――

THE EXAMPLES given in the last chapter will have conveyed to the reader the fact that the first step toward getting rich is to convey the idea of your wants to the Formless Substance.

This is true, and you will see that, in order to do so, it becomes necessary to relate yourself to the Formless Intelligence in a harmonious way.

To secure this harmonious relation is a matter of such primary and vital importance that I shall give some space to its discussion here and give you instructions which, if you will follow them, will be certain to bring you into perfect unity of mind with God.

The whole process of mental adjustment and atonement can be summed up in one word: gratitude.

First, you believe that there is one Intelligent Substance, from which all things proceed; second, you believe that this Substance gives you everything you desire; and third, you relate yourself to it by a feeling of deep and profound gratitude.

Many people who order their lives rightly in all other ways are kept in poverty by their lack of gratitude. Having received one gift from God, they cut the wires which connect them with Him by failing to make acknowledgment.

It is easy to understand that the nearer we live to the source of wealth the more wealth we shall receive; and it is easy also to understand that the soul that is always grateful lives in closer touch with God than the one which never looks to Him in thankful acknowledgment.

The more gratefully we fix our minds on the Supreme when good things come to us, the more good things we will receive, and the more rapidly they will come; and the reason simply is that the mental attitude of gratitude draws the mind into closer touch with the source from which the blessings come.

If it is a new thought to you that gratitude brings your whole mind into closer harmony with the creative energies of the universe, consider it well, and you will see that it is true. The good things you already have, have come to you along the line of obedience to certain laws. Gratitude will lead your mind out along the ways by which things come; and it will keep you in close harmony with creative thought and prevent you from falling into competitive thought.

Gratitude alone can keep you looking toward the All and prevent you from falling into the error of thinking of the supply as limited; to do that would be fatal to your hopes.

There is a Law of Gratitude, and it is absolutely necessary that you should observe the law if you are to get the results you seek.

The law of gratitude is the natural principle that action and reaction are always equal and in opposite directions.

The grateful outreaching of your mind in thankful praise to the Supreme *is a liberation or expenditure of force; it cannot fail to reach that to which it addressed, and the reaction is an instantaneous movement towards you.*

"Draw nigh unto God, and He will draw nigh unto you."
That is a statement of psychological truth.

And if your gratitude is strong and constant, the reaction in
Formless Substance will be strong and continuous; the movement of the things you want will be always toward you. Notice
the grateful attitude that Jesus took; how He always seems to
be saying, "I thank Thee, Father, that Thou hearest me." You
cannot exercise much power without gratitude; for it is gratitude that keeps you connected with Power.

But the value of gratitude does not consist solely in getting you more blessings in the future. Without gratitude, you
cannot long keep from dissatisfied thought regarding things
as they are.

The moment you permit your mind to dwell with dissatisfaction upon things as they are, you begin to lose ground.
You fix attention upon the common, the ordinary, the poor,
and the squalid and mean; and your mind takes the form of
these things. Then you will transmit these forms or mental images to the Formless, and the common, the poor, the
squalid, and mean will come to you.

To permit your mind to dwell upon the inferior is to become inferior and to surround yourself with inferior things.

On the other hand, to fix your attention on the best is to
surround yourself with the best and to become the best.

The Creative Power within us makes us into the image of
that to which we give our attention. We are Thinking Substance, and Thinking Substance always takes the form of that
which it thinks about.

The grateful mind is constantly fixed upon the best;
therefore, it tends to become the best; it takes the form or
character of the best and will receive the best.

Also, faith is born of gratitude. The grateful mind continually expects good things, and expectation becomes faith. The reaction of gratitude upon one's own mind produces faith; and every outgoing wave of grateful thanksgiving increases faith. He who has no feeling of gratitude cannot long retain a living faith; and, without a living faith, you cannot get rich by the creative method, as we shall see in the following chapters.

It is necessary, then, to cultivate the habit of being grateful for every good thing that comes to you and to give thanks continuously.

Because all things have contributed to your advancement, you should include all things in your gratitude.

Do not waste time thinking or talking about the shortcomings or wrong actions of plutocrats or trust magnates. Their organization of the world has made your opportunity; all you get really comes to you because of them.

Do not rage against corrupt politicians; if it were not for politicians, we should fall into anarchy, and your opportunity would be greatly lessened.

God has worked a long time and very patiently to bring us up to where we are in industry and government, and He is going right on with His work. There is not the least doubt that He will do away with plutocrats, trust magnates, captains of industry, and politicians as soon as they can be spared; but, in the meantime, behold they are all very good. Remember that they are all helping to arrange the lines of transmission along which your riches will come to you, and be grateful to them all. This will bring you into harmonious relations with the good in everything, and the good in everything will move toward you.

8. THINKING IN THE
CERTAIN WAY

———————— ⚜ ————————

TURN BACK to the sixth chapter, HOW RICHES COME TO YOU, and read again the story of the man who formed a mental image of his house, and you will get a fair idea of the initial step toward getting rich. You must form a clear and definite mental picture of what you want; you cannot transmit an idea unless you have it yourself.

You must have it before you can give it; and many people fail to impress Thinking Substance because they have only a vague and misty concept of the things they want to do, to have, or to become.

It is not enough that you should have a general desire for wealth "to do good with"; everybody has that desire.

It is not enough that you should have a wish to travel, see things, live more, etc. Everybody has those desires also. If you were going to send a wireless message to a friend, you would not send the letters of the alphabet in their order and let him construct the message for himself; nor would you take words at random from the dictionary. You would send a coherent sentence; one which meant something. When you try to impress your wants upon Substance, remember that it must be done by a coherent statement; you must know what you want and be definite. You can never get rich, or start the creative power into action, by sending out unformed longings and vague desires.

Go over your desires just as the man I have described went over his house; see just what you want, and get a clear mental picture of it as you wish it to look when you get it.

That clear mental picture you must have continually in mind, as the sailor has in mind the port toward which he is sailing the ship; you must keep your face toward it all the time. You must no more lose sight of it than the steersman loses sight of the compass.

It is not necessary to take exercises in concentration, nor to set apart special times for prayer and affirmation, nor to "go into the silence," nor to do occult stunts of any kind. These things are well enough, but all you need is to know what you want and to want it badly enough so that it will stay in your thoughts.

Spend as much of your leisure time as you can in contemplating your picture, but no one needs to exercise to concentrate his mind on a thing which he really wants; it is the things you do not really care about which require effort to fix your attention upon them.

And unless you really want to get rich and the desire is strong enough to hold your thoughts directed to the purpose as the magnetic pole holds the needle of the compass, it will hardly be worthwhile for you to try to carry out the instructions given in this book.

The methods set forth herein are for people whose desire for riches is strong enough to overcome mental laziness and the love of ease, and make them work.

The more clear and definite you make your picture then, and the more you dwell upon it, bringing out all its delightful details, the stronger your desire will be; and the stronger your desire, the easier it will be to hold your mind fixed upon the picture of what you want.

Something more is necessary, however, than merely to see the picture clearly. If that is all you do, you are only a dreamer and have little or no power for accomplishment.

Behind your clear vision must be the purpose to realize it; to bring it out in tangible expression.

And behind this purpose must be an invincible and unwavering *faith* that the thing is already yours; that it is "at hand" and you have only to take possession of it.

Live in the new house, mentally, until it takes form around you physically. In the mental realm, enter at once into full enjoyment of the things you want.

"Whatsoever things ye ask for when ye pray, believe that ye receive them, and ye shall have them," said Jesus.

See the things you want as if they were actually around you all the time; see yourself as owning and using them. Make use of them in imagination, just as you will use them when they are your tangible possessions. Dwell upon your mental picture until it is clear and distinct, and then take the Mental Attitude of Ownership toward everything in that picture. Take possession of it in mind, in the full faith that it is actually yours. Hold to this mental ownership; do not waiver for an instant in the faith that it is real.

And remember what was said in a proceeding chapter about gratitude; be as thankful for it all the time as you expect to be when it has taken form. The man who can sincerely thank God for the things which, as yet, he owns only in imagination has real faith. He will get rich; he will cause the creation of whatsoever he wants.

You do not need to pray repeatedly for things you want; it is not necessary to tell God about it every day.

"Use not vain repetitions as the heathens do," said Jesus to his pupils, "for your Father knoweth that ye have need of these things before ye ask Him."

Your part is to intelligently formulate your desire for the things which make for a larger life, to get these desires arranged into a coherent whole, and then to impress this Whole Desire upon the Formless Substance, which has the power and the will to bring you what you want.

You do not make this impression by repeating strings of words; you make it by holding the vision with unshakable *purpose* to attain it and with steadfast *faith* that you do attain it.

The answer to prayer is not according to your faith while you are talking, but according to your faith while you are working.

You cannot impress the mind of God by having a special Sabbath day set apart to tell Him what you want and then forgetting Him during the rest of the week. You cannot impress Him by having special hours to go into your closet and pray if you then dismiss the matter from your mind until the hour of prayer comes again.

Oral prayer is well enough and has its effect, especially upon yourself, in clarifying your vision and strengthening your faith; but it is not your oral petitions which get you what you want. In order to get rich, you do not need a "sweet hour of prayer"; you need to "pray without ceasing." And by prayer, I mean holding steadily to your vision with the purpose to cause its creation into solid form and the faith that you are doing so.

"Believe that ye receive them."

The whole matter turns on receiving, once you have clearly formed your vision. When you have formed it, it is well to make an oral statement, addressing the Supreme in reverent prayer; and, from that moment, you must, in mind, receive what you ask for. Live in the new house; wear the fine clothes; ride in the automobile; go on the journey and confidently plan for greater journeys. Think and speak of all the things you have asked for in terms of actual present ownership. Imagine an environment and a financial condition exactly as you want them, and live all the time in that imaginary environment and financial condition. Mind, however, that you do not do this as a mere dreamer and castle builder; hold to the *faith* that the imaginary is being realized and to the *purpose* to realize it. Remember that it is faith and purpose in the use of the imagination which makes the difference between the scientist and the dreamer. And having learned this fact, it is here that you must learn the proper use of the Will.

9. HOW TO USE THE WILL

⚜

TO SET about getting rich in a scientific way, you do not try to apply your willpower to anything outside of yourself.

You have no right to do so anyway.

It is wrong to apply your will to others in order to get them to do what you wish done.

It is as flagrantly wrong to coerce people by mental power as it is to coerce them by physical power. If compelling people by physical force to do things for you reduces them to slavery, compelling them by mental means accomplishes exactly the same thing; the only difference is in methods. If taking things from people by physical force is robbery, then taking things by mental force is robbery also; there is no difference in principle.

You have no right to use your willpower upon another person, even "for his own good"; for you do not know what is for his good. The Science of Getting Rich does not require you to apply power or force to any other person, in any way whatsoever. There is not the slightest necessity for doing so; indeed, any attempt to use your will upon others will only tend to defeat your purpose.

You do not need to apply your will to things in order to compel them to come to you. That would simply be trying to coerce God and would be foolish and useless, as well as irreverent.

You do not have to compel God to give you good things any more than you have to use your willpower to make the sun rise. You do not have to use your willpower to conquer an unfriendly deity or to make stubborn and rebellious forces do your bidding.

Substance is friendly to you and is more anxious to give you what you want than you are to get it. To get rich, you need only to use your willpower upon yourself.

When you know what to think and do, then you must use your will to compel yourself to think and do the right things. That is the legitimate use of the will in getting what you want—to use it in holding yourself to the right course. Use your will to keep yourself thinking and acting in the Certain Way.

Do not try to project your will, your thoughts, or your mind out into space to "act" on things or people. Keep your mind at home; it can accomplish more there than elsewhere. Use your mind to form a mental image of what you want and to hold that vision with faith and purpose; use your will to keep your mind working in the Right Way.

The more steady and continuous your faith and purpose, the more rapidly you will get rich because you will make only *positive* impressions upon Substance; and you will not neutralize or offset them by negative impressions.

The picture of your desires, held with faith and purpose, is taken up by the Formless and permeates it to great distances—throughout the universe for all I know.

As this impression spreads, all things are set moving toward its realization; every living thing, every inanimate thing, and the things yet uncreated are stirred toward bringing into being that which you want. All force begins to be exerted in that direction; all things begin to move toward you. The minds of people everywhere are influenced toward doing the things necessary to the fulfilling of your desires; and they work for you unconsciously.

But you can check all this by starting a negative impression in the Formless Substance. Doubt or unbelief is as certain to start a movement away from you as faith and purpose are to start one toward you. It is by not understanding this that most people who try to make use of "mental science" in getting rich make their failure. Every hour and moment you spend in giving heed to doubts and fears, every hour you spend in worry, every hour in which your soul is possessed by unbelief sets a current away from you in the whole domain of intelligent Substance. All the promises are unto them that believe and unto them only. Notice how insistent Jesus was upon this point of belief; and now you know the reason why.

Since belief is all important, it behooves you to guard your thoughts; and as your beliefs will be shaped to a very great extent by the things you observe and think about, it is important that you should command your attention.

And here the will comes into use; for it is by your will that you determine upon what things your attention shall be fixed.

If you want to become rich, you must not make a study of poverty.

Things are not brought into being by thinking about their opposites. Health is never to be attained by studying disease and thinking about disease; righteousness is not to be promoted by studying sin and thinking about sin; and no one ever got rich by studying poverty and thinking about poverty.

Medicine as a science of disease has increased disease, religion as a science of sin has promoted sin, and economics as a study of poverty will fill the world with wretchedness and want.

Do not talk about poverty; do not investigate it, or concern yourself with it. Never mind what its causes are; you have nothing to do with them. What concerns you is the cure.

Do not spend your time in charitable work or charity movements; all charity only tends to perpetuate the wretchedness it aims to eradicate.

I do not say that you should be hardhearted or unkind and refuse to hear the cry of need; but you must not try to eradicate poverty in any of the conventional ways. Put poverty behind you, and put all that pertains to it behind you and "make good." Get rich; that is the best way you can help the poor.

And you cannot hold the mental image which is to make you rich if you fill your mind with pictures of poverty. Do not read books or papers which give circumstantial accounts of the wretchedness of the tenement dwellers, of the horrors of child labor, and so on. Do not read anything which fills your mind with gloomy images of want and suffering.

You cannot help the poor in the least by knowing about these things; and the widespread knowledge of them does not tend at all to do away with poverty.

What tends to do away with poverty is, not the getting of pictures of poverty into your mind but, getting pictures of wealth into the minds of the poor.

You are not deserting the poor in their misery when you refuse to allow your mind to be filled with pictures of that misery.

Poverty can be done away with, not by increasing the number of well-to-do people who think about poverty but, by increasing the number of poor people who decide with purpose and faith to get rich.

The poor do not need charity; they need inspiration. Charity only sends them a loaf of bread to keep them alive in their wretchedness or gives them an entertainment to make them forget for an hour or two; but inspiration will cause them to rise out of their misery. If you want to help the poor, demonstrate to them that they can become rich; prove it by getting rich yourself.

The only way poverty will ever be banished from this world is by getting a large and constantly increasing number of people to practice the teachings of this book.

People must be taught to become rich by creation, not by competition.

Every man who becomes rich by competition throws down behind him the ladder by which he rises and keeps others down; but every man who gets rich by creation opens a way for thousands to follow him and inspires them to do so.

You are not showing hardness of heart or an unfeeling disposition when you refuse to pity poverty, see poverty, read about poverty, think or talk about it, or to listen to those who do talk about it. Use your will power to keep your mind *off* the subject of poverty and to keep it fixed with faith and purpose *on* the vision of what you want.

10. FURTHER USE
OF THE WILL

———— ⚜ ————

YOU CANNOT retain a true and clear vision of wealth if you are constantly turning your attention to opposing pictures, whether they be external or imaginary.

Do not tell of your past troubles of a financial nature; if you have had them, do not think of them at all. Do not tell of the poverty of your parents or the hardships of your early life; to do any of these things is to mentally class yourself with the poor, and it will certainly check the movement of things in your direction.

"Let the dead bury their dead," as Jesus said.

Put poverty and all things that pertain to poverty completely behind you.

You have accepted a certain theory of the universe as being correct and are resting all your hopes of happiness on its being correct; and what can you gain by giving heed to conflicting theories?

Do not read religious books which tell you that the world is soon coming to an end; and do not read the writing of muck-rakers and pessimistic philosophers who tell you that it is going to the devil.

The world is not going to the devil; it is going to God. It is wonderful Becoming.

True, there may be a good many things in existing conditions which are disagreeable; but what is the use of studying them when they are certainly passing away, and when the study of them only tends to check their passing and keep them with us? Why give time and attention to things which are being removed by evolutionary growth, when you can hasten their removal only by promoting the evolutionary growth as far as your part of it goes?

No matter how horrible the conditions in certain countries, sections, or places may seem, you waste your time and destroy your own chances by considering them.

You should interest yourself in the world's becoming rich.

Think of the riches the world is coming into, instead of the poverty it is growing out of; and bear in mind that the only way in which you can assist the world in growing rich is by growing rich yourself through the creative method—not the competitive one.

Give your attention wholly to riches; ignore poverty.

Whenever you think or speak of those who are poor, think and speak of them as those who are becoming rich; as those who are to be congratulated rather than pitied. Then, they and others will catch the inspiration and begin to search for the way out.

Because I say that you are to give your whole time and mind and thought to riches, it does not follow that you are to be sordid or mean.

To become really rich is the noblest aim you can have in life, for it includes everything else. On the competitive plane, the struggle to get rich is a God-less scramble for power over other men; but when we come into the creative mind, all this is changed.

All that is possible in the way of greatness and soul unfoldment, of service and lofty endeavor, comes by way of getting rich; all is made possible by the use of things.

If you lack for physical health, you will find that the attainment of it is conditional on your getting rich.

Only those who are emancipated from financial worry and who have the means to live a carefree existence and follow hygienic practices can have and retain health.

Moral and spiritual greatness is possible only to those who are above the competitive battle for existence; and only those who are becoming rich on the plane of creative thought are free from the degrading influences of competition. If your heart is set on domestic happiness, remember that love flourishes best where there is refinement, a high level of thought, and freedom from corrupt influences; and these are to be found only where riches are attained by the exercise of creative thought, without strife or rivalry.

You can aim at nothing so great or noble, I repeat, as to become rich; and you must fix your attention upon your mental picture of riches, to the exclusion of all that may tend to dim or obscure the vision.

You must learn to see the underlying *truth* in all things; you must see beneath all seemingly wrong conditions the Great One Life ever moving forward toward fuller expression and more complete happiness.

It is the truth that there is no such thing as poverty; there is only wealth.

Some people remain in poverty because they are ignorant of the fact that there is wealth for them; and these can best be taught by showing them the way to affluence in your own person and practice.

Others are poor because, while they feel that there is a way out, they are too intellectually indolent to put forth the mental effort necessary to find that way and travel by it; and for these, the very best thing you can do is to arouse their desire by showing them the happiness that comes from being rightly rich.

Others still are poor because, while they have some notion of science, they have become so swamped and lost in the maze of metaphysical and occult theories that they do not know which road to take. They try a mixture of many systems and fail in all. For these, again, the very best thing to do is to show the right way in your own person and practice; an ounce of doing things is worth a pound of theorizing.

The very best thing you can do for the whole world is to make the most of yourself.

You can serve God and man in no more effective way than by getting rich; that is, if you get rich by the creative method and not by the competetive one.

Another thing. We assert that this book gives in detail the principles of The Science of Getting Rich; and if that is true, you do not need to read any other book upon the subject. This may sound narrow and egotistical, but consider: there is no more scientific method of computation in mathematics than by addition, subtraction, multiplication, and division; no other method is possible. There can be but one shortest distance between two points. There is only one way to think scientifically, and that is to think in the way that leads by the most direct and simple route to the goal. No man has yet formulated a briefer or less complex "system" than the one set forth herein; it has been stripped of all nonessentials. When you commence on this, lay all others aside; put them out of your mind altogether.

Read this book every day; keep it with you; commit it to memory, and do not think about other "systems" and theories. If you do, you will begin to have doubts and to be uncertain and wavering in your thought; and then you will begin to make failures.

After you have made good and become rich, you may study other systems as much as you please; but until you are quite sure that you have gained what you want, do not read anything along this line but this book, unless it be the authors mentioned in the preface.

And read only the most optimistic comments on the world's news; those in harmony with your picture.

Also, postpone your investigations into the occult. Do not dabble in theosophy, Spiritualism, or kindred studies. It is very likely that the dead still live and are near; but if they are, let them alone; mind your own business.

Wherever the spirits of the dead may be, they have their own work to do and their own problems to solve; and we have no right to interfere with them. We cannot help them, and it is very doubtful whether they can help us or whether we have any right to trespass upon their time if they can. Let the dead and the hereafter alone, and solve your own problem; get rich. If you begin to mix with the occult, you will start mental cross-currents which will surely bring your hopes to shipwreck. Now, this and the preceding chapters have brought us to the following statement of basic facts:

There is a thinking stuff from which all things are made and which, in its original state, permeates, penetrates, and fills the interspaces of the universe.

A thought, in this substance, produces the thing that is imaged by the thought.

Man can form things in his thought and, by impressing his thought upon formless substance, can cause the thing he thinks about to be created.

In order to do this, man must pass from the competitive to the creative mind; he must form a clear mental picture of the things he wants and hold this picture in his thoughts with the fixed purpose *to get what he wants and the unwavering* faith *that he does get what he wants, closing his mind against all that may tend to shake his purpose, dim his vision, or quench his faith.*

And in addition to all this, we shall now see that he must live and act in a Certain Way.

11. ACTING IN THE CERTAIN WAY

———— ⚜ ————

THOUGHT IS the creative power, or the impelling force, which causes the creative power to act; thinking in a Certain Way will bring riches to you, but you must not rely upon thought alone, paying no attention to personal action. That is the rock upon which many otherwise scientific, metaphysical thinkers meet shipwreck—the failure to connect thought with personal action.

We have not yet reached the stage of development, even supposing such a stage to be possible, in which man can create directly from Formless Substance without nature's processes or the work of human hands; man must not only think, but his personal action must supplement his thought.

By thought, you can cause the gold in the hearts of the mountains to be impelled toward you; but it will not mine itself, refine itself, coin itself into double eagles, and come rolling along the roads seeking its way into your pocket.

Under the impelling power of the Supreme Spirit, men's affairs will be so ordered that someone will be led to mine the gold for you; other men's business transactions will be so directed that the gold will be brought toward you, and you must so arrange your own business affairs that you may be able to receive it when it comes to you. Your thought makes all things, animate and inanimate, work to bring you what you want; but your personal activity must be such that you can rightly receive what you want when it reaches you. You are not to take it as charity, nor to steal it; you must give every man more in use value than he gives you in cash value.

The scientific use of thought consists of forming a clear and distinct mental image of what you want, holding fast to the purpose to get what you want, and realizing with grateful faith that you do get what you want.

Do not try to "project" your thought in any mysterious or occult way, with the idea of having it go out and do things for you; that is wasted effort and will weaken your power to think with sanity.

The action of thought in getting rich is fully explained in the preceding chapters; your faith and purpose positively impress your vision upon Formless Substance, which has *the same desire for more life that you have*; and this vision, received from you, sets all the creative forces at work *in and through their regular channels of action* but directed toward you.

It is not your part to guide or supervise the creative process; all you have to do with that is to retain your vision, stick to your purpose, and maintain your faith and gratitude.

But you must act in a Certain Way, so that you can appropriate what is yours when it comes to you, so that you can meet the things you have in your picture and put them in their proper places as they arrive.

You can really see the truth of this. When things reach you, they will be in the hands of other men who will ask an equivalent for them.

And you can only get what is yours by giving the other man what is his.

Your pocketbook is not going to be transformed into a Fortunata's purse, which shall be always full of money without effort on your part.

This is the crucial point in the Science of Getting Rich, right here, where thought and personal action must be combined. There are very many people who, consciously or unconsciously, set the creative forces in action by the strength and persistence of their desires, but who remain poor because they do not provide for the reception of the thing they want when it comes.

By thought, the thing you want is brought to you; by action, you receive it.

Whatever your action is to be, it is evident that you must act *now*. You cannot act in the past, and it is essential to the clearness of your mental vision that you dismiss the past from your mind. You cannot act in the future, for the future is not here yet. And you cannot tell how you will want to act in any future contingency until that contingency has arrived.

Because you are not in the right business or the right environment now, do not think that you must postpone action until you get into the right business or environment. And do not spend time in the present taking thought as to the best course in possible future emergencies; have faith in your ability to meet any emergency when it arrives.

If you act in the present, with your mind on the future, your present action will be with a divided mind and will not be effective.

Put your whole mind into present action. Do not give your creative impulse to Original Substance and then sit down and wait for results; if you do, you will never get them. Act now. There is never any time but now, and there never will be any time but now. If you are ever to begin to make ready for the reception of what you want, you must begin now.

And your action, whatever it is, must most likely be in your present business or employment and must be upon the persons and things in your present environment.

You cannot act where you are not, you cannot act where you have been, and you cannot act where you are going to be; you can act only where you are.

Do not bother as to whether yesterday's work was well done or ill done; do today's work well. Do not try to do tomorrow's work now; there will be plenty of time to do that when you get to it. Do not try, by occult or mystical means, to act on people or things that are out of your reach. Do not wait for a change of environment before you act; get a change of environment by action.

You can so act upon the environment in which you are now as to cause yourself to be transferred to a better environment.

Hold with faith and purpose the vision of yourself in the better environment, but act upon your present environment with all your heart, and with all your strength, and with all your mind.

Do not spend any time in daydreaming or castle building; hold to the one vision of what you want, and act *now*.

Do not cast about seeking some new thing to do, or some strange, unusual, or remarkable action to perform as a first step toward getting rich. It is probable that your actions, at least for some time to come, will be those you have been performing for some time past; but you are to begin now to perform these actions in the Certain Way, which will surely make you rich.

If you are engaged in some business, and feel that it is not the right one for you, do not wait until you get into the right business before you begin to act.

Do not feel discouraged or sit down and lament because you are misplaced. No man was ever so misplaced but that he could not find the right place, and no man ever became so involved in the wrong business but that he could get into the right business.

Hold the vision of yourself in the right business, with the purpose to get into it, and the faith that you will get into it and are getting into it; but *act* in your present business. Use your present business as the means of getting a better one, and use your present enviornment as the means of getting into a better one. Your vision of the right business, if held with faith and purpose, will cause the Supreme to move the right business toward you; and your action, if performed in the Certain Way, will cause you to move toward the business.

If you are an employee, or wage earner, and feel that you must change places in order to get what you want, do not "project" your thought into space and rely upon it to get you another job. It will probably fail to do so.

Hold the vision of yourself in the job you want, while you *act* with faith and purpose on the job you have, and you will certainly get the job you want.

Your vision and faith will set the creative force in motion to bring it toward you, and your action will cause the forces in your own environment to move you toward the place you want. In closing this chapter, we will add another statement to our syllabus:

There is a thinking stuff from which all things are made and which, in its original state, permeates, penetrates, and fills the interspaces of the universe.

A thought, in this substance, produces the thing that is imaged by the thought.

Man can form things in his thought and, by impressing his thought upon formless substance, can cause the thing he thinks about to be created.

In order to do this, man must pass from the competitive to the creative mind; he must form a clear mental picture of the things he wants and hold this picture in his thoughts with the fixed purpose *to get what he wants and the unwavering* faith *that he does get what he wants, closing his mind against all that may tend to shake his purpose, dim his vision, or quench his faith.*

That he may receive what he wants when it comes, man must act now *upon the people and things in his present environment.*

I2. EFFICIENT ACTION

— ⚜ —

YOU MUST use your thought as directed in previous chapters and begin to do what you can do where you are; and you must do *all* that you can do where you are.

You can advance only by being larger than your present place; and no man is larger than his present place who leaves undone any of the work pertaining to that place.

The world is advanced only by those who more than fill their present places.

If no man quite filled his present place, you can see that there must be a going backward in everything. Those who do not quite fill their present places are dead weight upon society, government, commerce, and industry; they must be carried along by others at a great expense. The progress of the world is retarded only by those who do not fill the places they are holding; they belong to a former age and a lower stage or plane of life, and their tendency is toward degeneration. No society could advance if every man was smaller than his place; social evolution is guided by the law of physical and mental evolution. In the animal world, evolution is caused by excess of life.

When an organism has more life than can be expressed in the functions of its own plane, it develops the organs of a higher plane, and a new species is originated.

There never would have been new species had there not been organisms which more than filled their places. The law is exactly the same for you; getting rich depends upon your applying this principle to your own affairs.

Every day is either a successful day or a day of failure; and it is the successful days which get you what you want. If every day is a failure, you can never get rich; while if every day is a success, you cannot fail to get rich.

If there is something that may be done today, and you do not do it, you have failed insofar as that thing is concerned; and the consequences may be more disastrous than you imagine.

You cannot foresee the results of even the most trivial act; you do not know the workings of all the forces that have been set moving in your behalf. Much may be depending on your doing some simple act; it may be the very thing which is to open the door of opportunity to great possibilities. You can never know all the combinations which Supreme Intelligence is making for you in the world of things and of human affairs; your neglect or failure to do some small thing may cause a long delay in getting what you want.

Do, every day, *all* that can be done that day.

There is, however, a limitation or qualification of the above that you must take into account.

You are not to overwork, nor to rush blindly into your business in the effort to do the greatest possible number of things in the shortest possible time.

You are not to try to do tomorrow's work today, nor to do a week's work in a day.

It is really not the number of things you do, but the efficiency of each separate action that counts.

Every act is, in itself, either a success or a failure.

Every act is, in itself, either efficient or inefficient.

Every inefficient act is a failure, and if you spend your life in doing inefficient acts, your whole life will be a failure. The more things you do, the worse for you, if all your acts are inefficient ones.

On the other hand, every efficient act is a success in itself, and if every act of your life is an efficient one, your whole life *must* be a success.

The cause of failure is doing too many things in an inefficient manner and not doing enough things in an efficient manner.

You will see that it is a self-evident proposition that, if you do not do any inefficient acts, and if you do a sufficient number of efficient acts, you will become rich. If, now, it is possible for you to make each act an efficient one, you see again that the getting of riches is reduced to an exact science, like mathematics.

The matter turns, then, on the question of whether you can make each separate act a success in itself. And this you can certainly do.

You can make each act a success because *all* Power is working with you; and *all* Power cannot fail.

Power is at your service; and to make each act efficient, you have only to put power into it.

Every action is either strong or weak; and when every one is strong, you are acting in the Certain Way which will make you rich.

Every act can be made strong and efficient by holding

your vision while you are doing it, and putting the whole power of your *faith* and *purpose* into it.

It is at this point that the people who separate mental power from personal action fail. They use the power of mind in one place and at one time, and they act in another place and at another time, so their acts are not successful in themselves; too many of them are inefficient. But if *all* Power goes into every act, no matter how commonplace, every act will be a success in itself; and, as is the nature of things, every success opens the way to other successes. Your progress toward what you want and the progress of what you want toward you will become increasingly rapid.

Remember that successful action is cumulative in its results. Since the desire for more life is inherent in all things, when a man begins to move toward larger life, more things attach themselves to him, and the influence of his desire is multiplied.

Do, every day, all that you can do that day, and do each act in an efficient manner.

In saying that you must hold your vision while you are doing each act, however trivial or commonplace, I do not mean to say that it is necessary at all times to see the vision distinctly to its smallest details. It should be the work of your leisure hours to use your imagination on the details of your vision and to contemplate them until they are firmly fixed upon memory. If you wish speedy results, spend practically all your spare time in this practice.

By continuous contemplation you will get the picture of what you want, even to the smallest details, so firmly fixed upon your mind and so completely transferred to the mind of Formless Substance, that in your working hours you need only to mentally refer to the picture to stimulate your faith and purpose and cause your best effort to be put forth. Contemplate your picture in your leisure hours until your consciousness is so full of it that you can grasp it instantly. You will become so enthused with its bright promises that the mere thought of it will call forth the strongest energies of your whole being.

Let us again repeat our syllabus, and, by slightly changing the closing statements, bring it to the point we have now reached.

There is a thinking stuff from which all things are made and which, in its original state, permeates, penetrates, and fills the interspaces of the universe.

A thought, in this substance, produces the thing that is imaged by the thought.

Man can form things in his thought and, by impressing his thought upon formless substance, can cause the thing he thinks about to be created.

In order to do this, man must pass from the competitive to the creative mind; he must form a clear mental picture of the things he wants and do, with faith and purpose, all that can be done each day, doing each separate thing in an efficient manner.

13. GETTING INTO THE
RIGHT BUSINESS

———— ❧ ————

SUCCESS, IN any business, depends for one thing upon your possessing, in a well-developed state, the faculties required in that business.

Without good musical faculty, no one can succeed as a teacher of music; without well-developed mechanical faculties, no one can achieve great success in any of the mechanical trades; without tact and the commercial faculties, no one can succeed in mercantile pursuits. But to possess, in a well-developed state, the faculties required in your particular vocation does not ensure getting rich. There are musicians who have remarkable talent and who yet remain poor; there are blacksmiths, carpenters, and so on who have excellent mechanical ability, but who do not get rich; and there are merchants with good faculties for dealing with men who nevertheless fail.

The different faculties are tools; it is essential to have good tools, but it is also essential that the tools should be used in the Right Way. One man can take a sharp saw, a square, a good plane, and so on and build a handsome article of furniture; another man can take the same tools and set to work to duplicate the article, but his production will be a botch. He does not know how to use good tools in a successful way.

The various faculties of your mind are the tools with which you must do the work which is to make you rich; it will be easier for you to succeed if you get into a business for which you are well equipped with mental tools.

Generally speaking, you will do best in the business which will use your strongest faculties; the one for which you are naturally "best fitted." But there are limitations to this statement also. No man should regard his vocation as being irrevocably fixed by the tendencies with which he was born.

You can get rich in *any* business, for if you have not the right talent for it, you can develop that talent; it merely means that you will have to make your tools as you go along, instead of confining yourself to the use of those with which you were born. It will be *easier* for you to succeed in a vocation for which you already have the talents in a well-developed state; but you *can* succeed in any vocation, for you can develop any rudimentary talent, and there is no talent of which you have not at least the rudiment.

You will get rich most easily, in point of effort, if you do that for which you are best fitted; but you will get rich most satisfactorily if you do that which you *want* to do.

Doing what you want to do is life; and there is no real satisfaction in living if we are compelled to be forever doing something which we do not like to do and can never do what we want to do. And it is certain that you can do what you want to do; the *desire* to do it is proof that you have within you the power which *can* do it.

Desire is a manifestation of power.

The desire to play music is the power which can play music seeking expression and development; the desire to invent mechanical devices is the mechanical talent seeking expression and development.

Where there is no power, either developed or undeveloped, to do a thing, there is never any desire to do that thing; and where there is strong desire to do a thing, it is certain proof that the power to do it is strong and only requires to be developed and applied in the Right Way.

All things else being equal, it is best to select the business for which you have the best developed talent; but if you have a strong desire to engage in any particular line of work, you should select that work as the ultimate end at which you aim.

You can do what you want to do, and it is your right and privilege to follow the business or avocation which will be most congenial and pleasant.

You are not obliged to do what you do not like to do and should not do it except as a means to bring you to the doing of the thing you want to do.

If there are past mistakes whose consequences have placed you in an undesirable business or environment, you may be obliged for some time to do what you do not like to do; but you can make the doing of it pleasant by knowing that it is making it possible for you to come to the doing of what you want to do.

If you feel that you are not in the right vocation, do not act too hastily in trying to get into another one. The best way, generally, to change business or environment is by growth.

Do not be afraid to make a sudden and radical change if the opportunity is presented and you feel, after careful consideration, that it is the right opportunity; but never take sudden or radical action when you are in doubt as to the wisdom of doing so.

There is never any hurry on the creative plane; and there is no lack of opportunity.

When you get out of the competitive mind, you will understand that you never need to act hastily. No one else is going to beat you to the thing you want to do; there is enough for all. If one space is taken, another and a better one will be opened for you a little farther on; there is plenty of time. When you are in doubt, wait. Fall back on the contemplation of your vision, and increase your faith and purpose; and by all means, in times of doubt and indecision, cultivate gratitude.

A day or two spent in contemplating the vision of what you want, and in earnest thanksgiving that you are getting it, will bring your mind into such close relationship with the Supreme that you will make no mistake when you act.

There is a mind which knows all there is to know; and you can come into close unity with this mind by faith and the purpose to advance in life if you have deep gratitude.

Mistakes come from acting hastily, or from acting in fear or doubt, or in forgetfulness of the Right Motive, which is more life to all and less to none.

As you go on in the Certain Way, opportunities will come to you in increasing number; and you will need to be very steady in your faith and purpose and to keep in close touch with the All Mind by reverent gratitude.

Do all that you can do in a perfect manner every day, but do it without haste, worry, or fear. Go as fast as you can, but never hurry.

Remember that in the moment you begin to hurry, you cease to be a creator and become a competitor; you drop back upon the old plane again.

Whenever you find yourself hurrying, call a halt; fix your attention on the mental image of the thing you want, and begin to give thanks that you are getting it. The exercise of *gratitude* will never fail to strengthen your faith and renew your purpose.

14. THE IMPRESSION
OF INCREASE

————— ⚜ —————

WHETHER YOU change your vocation or not, your actions for the present must be those pertaining to the business in which you are now engaged.

You can get into the business you want by making constructive use of the business you are already established in; by doing your daily work in a Certain Way.

And insofar as your business consists in dealing with other men, whether personally or by letter, the key-thought of all your efforts must be to convey to their minds the impression of increase.

Increase is what all men and all women are seeking; it is the urge of the Formless Intelligence within them, seeking fuller expression.

The desire for increase is inherent in all nature; it is the fundamental impulse of the universe. All human activities are based on the desire for increase; people are seeking more food, more clothes, better shelter, more luxury, more beauty, more knowledge, more pleasure—increase in something equals more life.

Every living thing is under this necessity for continuous advancement; where increase of life ceases, dissolution and death set in at once.

Man instinctively knows this, and hence, he is forever seeking more. This law of perpetual increase is set forth by Jesus in the parable of the talents; only those who gain more retain any; "From him who hath not shall be taken away even that which he hath."

The normal desire for increased wealth is not an evil or a reprehensible thing; it is simply the desire for more abundant life; it is aspiration.

And because it is the deepest instinct of their natures, all men and women are attracted to Him who can give them more of the means of life.

In following the Certain Way as described in the foregoing pages, you are getting continuous increase, and you are giving it to all with whom you deal.

You are a creative center, from which increase is given off to all.

Be sure of this, and convey assurance of the fact to every man, woman, and child with whom you come in contact. No matter how small the transaction, even if it be only the selling of a stick of candy to a little child, put into it the thought of increase, and make sure that the customer is impressed with the thought.

Convey the impression of advancement with everything you do, so that all people shall receive the impression that you are an advancing man and that you advance all who deal with you. Even to the people whom you meet in a social way, without any thought of business and to whom you do not try to sell anything, give the thought of increase.

You can convey this impression by holding the unshakable faith that you are in the Way of Increase, and by letting this faith inspire, fill, and permeate every action.

Do everything that you do in the firm conviction that you are an advancing personality and that you are giving advancement to everybody.

Feel that you are getting rich, and, in so doing, you are making others rich and conferring benefits on all.

Do not boast or brag of your success or talk about it unnecessarily; true faith is never boastful.

Wherever you find a boastful person, you find one who is secretly doubtful and afraid. Simply feel the faith, and let it work out in every transaction; let every act and tone and look express the quiet assurance that you are getting rich, that you are already rich. Words will not be necessary to communicate this feeling to others; they will feel the sense of increase when in your presence and will be attracted to you again.

You must so impress others that they will feel that in associating with you they will get increase for themselves. See that you give them a use value greater than the cash value you are taking from them.

Take an honest pride in doing this, and let everybody know it; and you will have no lack of customers. People will go where they are given increase; and the Supreme, which desires increase in all and which knows all, will move toward you men and women who have never heard of you. Your business will increase rapidly, and you will be surprised at the unexpected benefits which will come to you. You will be able from day to day to make larger combinations, secure greater advantages, and to go on into a more congenial vocation if you desire to do so.

But doing all this, you must never lose sight of your vision of what you want or your faith and purpose to get what you want.

Let me here give you another word of caution in regard to motives.

Beware of the insidious temptation to seek for power over other men.

Nothing is so pleasant to the unformed or partially developed mind as the exercise of power or dominion over others. *The desire to rule for selfish gratification has been the curse of the world.* For countless ages, kings and lords have drenched the earth with blood in their battles to extend their dominions; this, not to seek more life for all but, to get more power for themselves.

Today, the main motive in the business and industrial world is the same; men marshal their armies of dollars and lay waste the lives and hearts of millions in the same mad scramble for power over others. Commercial kings, like political kings, are inspired by the lust for power.

Jesus saw in this desire for mastery the moving impulse of that evil world He sought to overthrow. Read the twenty-third chapter of Matthew, and see how He pictures the lust of the Pharisees to be called "Master," to sit in the high places, to domineer over others, and to lay burdens on the backs of the less fortunate; and note how He compares this lust for dominion with the brotherly seeking for the Common Good to which He calls His disciples.

Watch out for the temptation to seek for authority, to become a "master," to be considered as one who is above the common herd, to impress others by lavish display, and so on.

The mind that seeks for mastery over others is the competitive mind; and the competitive mind is not the creative one. In order to master your environment and your destiny, it is not at all necessary that you should rule over your fellow men and, indeed, when you fall into the world's struggle for the high places, you begin to be conquered by fate and environment, and your getting rich becomes a matter of chance and speculation.

Beware of the competitive mind. No better statement of the principle of creative action can be formulated than the favorite declaration of the late Samuel "Golden Rule" Jones of Toledo: "What I want for myself, I want for everybody."

15. THE ADVANCING MAN

⚜

WHAT I have said in the last chapter applies as well to the professional man and the wage earner as to the man who is engaged in mercantile business.

No matter whether you are a physician, a teacher, or a clergyman, if you can give increase of life to others and make them sensible of the fact, they will be attracted to you, and you will get rich. The physician who holds the vision of himself as a great and successful healer and who works toward the complete realization of that vision with faith and purpose, as described in former chapters, will come into such close touch with the Source of Life that he will be phenomenally successful; patients will come to him in throngs.

No one has a greater opportunity to carry into effect the teaching of this book than the practitioner of medicine; it does not matter to which of the various schools he may belong, for the principle of healing is common to all of them and may be reached by all alike. The advancing man in medicine, who holds to a clear mental image of himself as successful and who obeys the laws of faith, purpose, and gratitude, will cure every curable case he undertakes, no matter what remedies he may use.

In the field of religion, the world cries out for the clergyman who can teach his hearers the true science of abundant life. He who masters the details of *The Science of Getting Rich* together with the allied sciences of being well, of being great, and of winning love, and who teaches these details from the pulpit will never lack for a congregation. This is the gospel that the world needs; it will give increase of life, and men will hear it gladly and will give liberal support to the man who brings it to them.

What is now needed is a demonstration of the science of life from the pulpit. We want preachers who cannot only tell us how, but who in their own persons will show us how. We need the preacher who will himself be rich, healthy, great, and beloved to teach us how to attain these things; and when he comes, he will find a numerous and loyal following.

The same is true of the teacher who can inspire the children with the faith and purpose of the advancing life. He will never be out of a job. And any teacher who has this faith and purpose can give it to his pupils; he cannot help giving it to them if it is part of his own life and practice.

What is true of the teacher, preacher, and physician is true of the lawyer, dentist, real estate man, insurance agent—of everybody.

The combined mental and personal action I have described is infallible; it cannot fail. Every man and woman who follows these instructions steadily, perseveringly, and to the letter will get rich. The law of the Increase of Life is as mathematically certain in its operation as the law of gravity; getting rich is an exact science.

The wage earner will find this as true of his case as of

any of the others mentioned. Do not feel that you have no chance to get rich because you are working where there is no visible opportunity for advancement, where wages are small and the cost of living high. Form your clear mental vision of what you want, and begin to act with faith and purpose.

Do all the work you can do, every day, and do each piece of work in a perfectly successful manner; put the power of success, and the purpose to get rich, into everything that you do.

But do not do this merely with the idea of currying favor with your employer, in the hope that he, or those above you, will see your good work and advance you; it is not likely that they will do so.

The man who is merely a "good" workman, filling his place to the very best of his ability, and satisfied with that is valuable to his employer; and it is not to the employer's interest to promote him; he is worth more where he is.

To secure advancement, something more is necessary than to be too large for your place.

The man who is certain to advance is the one who is too big for his place, who has a clear concept of what he wants to be, who knows that he can become what he wants to be, and who is determined to *be* what he wants to be.

Do not try to more than fill your present place with a view to pleasing your employer; do it with the idea of advancing yourself. Hold the faith and purpose of increase during work hours, after work hours, and before work hours. Hold it in such a way that every person who comes in contact with you, whether foreman, fellow workman, or social acquaintance, will feel the power of purpose radiating from you; so that everyone will get the sense of advancement and increase from you. Men will be attracted to you, and if there is no possibility for advancement in your present job, you will very soon see an opportunity to take another job.

There is a Power which never fails to present opportunity to the advancing man who is moving in obedience to law.

God cannot help helping you if you act in a Certain Way; He must do so in order to help Himself.

There is nothing in your circumstances or in the industrial situation that can keep you down. If you cannot get rich working for the steel trust, you can get rich on a ten-acre farm; and if you begin to move in the Certain Way, you will certainly escape from the "clutches" of the steel trust and get on to the farm or wherever else you wish to be.

If a few thousand of its employees would enter upon the Certain Way, the steel trust would soon be in a bad plight; it would have to give its workingmen more opportunity or go out of business. Nobody has to work for a trust; the trusts can keep men in so called hopeless conditions only so long as there are men who are too ignorant to know of The Science of Getting Rich or too intellectually slothful to practice it.

Begin this way of thinking and acting, and your faith and purpose will make you quick to see any opportunity to better your condition.

Such opportunities will speedily come, for the Supreme, working in All and working for you, will bring them before you.

Do not wait for an opportunity to be all that you want to be; when an opportunity to be more than you are now is presented and you feel impelled toward it, take it. It will be the first step toward a greater opportunity.

There is no such thing possible in this universe as a lack of opportunities for the man who is living the advancing life.

It is inherent in the constitution of the cosmos that all things shall be for him and work together for his good; and he must certainly get rich if he acts and thinks in the Certain Way. So let wage earning men and women study this book with great care and enter with confidence upon the course of action it prescribes; it will not fail.

16. SOME CAUTIONS AND CONCLUDING OBSERVATIONS

———— ⚜ ————

MANY PEOPLE will scoff at the idea that there is an exact Science of Getting Rich; holding the impression that the supply of wealth is limited, they will insist that social and governmental institutions must be changed before considerable number of people can acquire a competence.

But this is not true.

It is true that existing governments keep the masses in poverty, but this is because the masses do not think and act in the Certain Way.

If the masses begin to move forward as suggested in this book, neither governments nor industrial systems can check them; all systems must be modified to accommodate the forward movement.

If the people have the advancing mind, have the Faith that they can become rich, and move forward with the fixed purpose to become rich nothing can possibly keep them in poverty.

Individuals may enter upon the Certain Way at any time and under any government, and make themselves rich; and when any considerable number of individuals do so under any government, they will cause the system to be so modified as to open the way for others.

The more men who get rich on the competitive plane, the worse for others; the more who get rich on the creative plane, the better for others.

The economic salvation of the masses can only be accomplished by getting a large number of people to practice the scientific method set down in this book and become rich. These will show others the way and inspire them with a desire for real life, with the faith that it can be attained and with the purpose to attain it.

For the present, however, it is enough to know that neither the government under which you live nor the capitalistic or competitive system of industry can keep you from getting rich. When you enter upon the creative plane of thought, you will rise above all these things and become a citizen of another kingdom.

But remember that your thought must be held upon the creative plane; you are never for an instant to be betrayed into regarding the supply as limited or into acting on the moral level of competition.

Whenever you do fall into old ways of thought, correct yourself instantly; when you are in the competitive mind, you have lost the cooperation of the mind of the Whole.

Do not spend any time in planning as to how you will meet possible emergencies in the future, except as the necessary policies may affect your actions today. You are concerned with doing today's work in a perfectly successful manner and not with emergencies which may arise tomorrow; you can attend to them as they come.

Do not concern yourself with questions as to how you

shall surmount obstacles which may loom upon your business horizon, unless you can see plainly that your course must be altered today in order to avoid them.

No matter how tremendous an obstruction may appear at a distance, you will find that, if you go on in the Certain Way, it will disappear as you approach it or a way over, through, or around it will appear.

No possible combination of circumstances can defeat a man or woman who is proceeding to get rich along strictly scientific lines. No man or woman who obeys the law can fail to get rich any more than one can multiply two by two and fail to get four.

Give no thought to possible disasters, obstacles, panics, or unfavorable combinations of circumstances; it is time enough to meet such things when they present themselves before you in the immediate present, and you will find that every difficulty carries with it the wherewithal for its overcoming.

Guard your speech. Never speak of yourself, your affairs, or of anything else in a discouraging way.

Never admit the possibility of failure or speak in a way that infers failure as a possibility.

Never speak of the times as being hard or of business conditions as being doubtful. Times may be hard and business doubtful for those who are on the competitive plane, but they can never be so for you; you can create what you want, and you are above fear.

When others are having hard times and poor business, you will find your greatest opportunities.

Train yourself to think of and to look upon the world as something which is Becoming, which is growing, and to regard seeming evil as being only that which is undeveloped.

Always speak in terms of advancement; to do otherwise is to deny your faith, and to deny your faith is to lose it.

Never allow yourself to feel disappointed. You may expect to have a certain thing at a certain time and not get it at that time; this will appear to you like failure.

But if you hold to your faith, you will find that the failure is only apparent.

Go on in the Certain Way, and if you do not receive that thing, you will receive something so much better that you will see that the seeming failure was really a success.

A student of this science had set his mind on making a certain business combination which seemed to him at the time to be very desirable, and he worked for some weeks to bring it about. When the crucial time came, the thing failed in a perfectly inexplicable way; it was as if some unseen influence had been working secretly against him. He was not disappointed; on the contrary, he thanked God that his desire had been overruled and went steadily on with a grateful mind. In a few weeks, an opportunity so much better came his way that he would not have made the first deal on any account; and he saw that a Mind which knew more than he knew had prevented him from losing the greater good by entangling himself with the lesser.

That is the way every seeming failure will work out for you if you keep your faith, hold to your purpose, have gratitude, and do, every day, all that can be done that day, doing each separate act in a successful manner.

When you make a failure, it is because you have not asked for enough; keep on, and a larger thing than you were seeking will certainly come to you. Remember this.

You will not fail because you lack the necessary talent to do what you wish to do. If you go on as I have directed, you will develop all the talent that is necessary to the doing of your work.

It is not within the scope of this book to deal with the science of cultivating talent; but it is as certain and simple as the process of getting rich.

However, do not hesitate or waver for fear that when you come to any certain place you will fail for lack of ability; keep right on, and when you come to that place, the ability will be furnished to you. The same source of ability which enabled the untaught Abraham Lincoln to do the greatest work in government ever accomplished by a single man is open to you; you may draw upon all the mind there is for wisdom to use in meeting the responsibilities which are laid upon you. Go on in full faith.

Study this book. Make it your constant companion until you have mastered all the ideas contained in it. While you are getting firmly established in this faith, you will do well to give up most recreations and pleasure and to stay away from places where ideas conflicting with these are advanced in lectures or sermons. Do not read pessimistic or conflicting literature or get into arguments upon the matter. Do very little reading outside of the writers mentioned in the preface. Spend most of your leisure time in contemplating your vision, in cultivating gratitude, and in reading this book. It contains all you need to know of the Science of Getting Rich; and you will find all the essentials summed up in the following chapter.

17. SUMMARY OF THE SCIENCE OF GETTING RICH

❧

THERE IS a Thinking Stuff from which all things are made and which, in its original state, permeates, penetrates, and fills the interspaces of the universe.

A thought in this substance produces the thing that is imaged by the thought.

Man can form things in his thought, and by impressing his thought upon Formless Substance can cause the thing he thinks about to be created.

To do this, man must pass from the competitive to the creative mind; otherwise, he cannot be in harmony with the Formless Intelligence, which is always creative and never competitive in spirit.

Man may come into full harmony with the Formless Substance by entertaining a lively and sincere gratitude for the blessings it bestows upon him. Gratitude unifies the mind of man with the intelligence of Substance, so that man's thoughts are received by the Formless. Man can remain upon the creative plane only by uniting himself with the Formless Intelligence through a deep and continuous feeling of gratitude.

Man must form a clear and definite mental image of the things he wishes to have, to do, or to become; and he must hold this mental image in his thoughts, while being deeply grateful to the Supreme that all his desires are granted to him. The man who wishes to get rich must spend his leisure hours in contemplating his Vision and in earnest thanksgiving that the reality is being given to him. Too much stress cannot be laid on the importance of frequent contemplation of the mental image, coupled with unwavering faith and devout gratitude. This is the process by which the impression is given to the Formless and the creative forces set in motion.

The Creative Energy works through the established channels of natural growth and of the industrial and social order. All that is included in his mental image will surely be brought to the man who follows the instructions given above and whose faith does not waver. What he wants will come to him through the ways of established trade and commerce.

In order to receive his own when it shall come to him, man must be active; and this activity can only consist in more than filling his present place. He must keep in mind the Purpose to get rich through the realization of his mental image. And he must do, every day, all that can be done that day, taking care to do each act in a successful manner. He must give to every man a use value in excess of the cash value he receives, so that each transaction makes for more life; and he must so hold the Advancing Thought that the impression of increase will be communicated to all with whom he comes in contact.

The men and women who practice these instructions will certainly get rich; and the riches they receive will be in exact proportion to the definiteness of their vision, the fixity of their purpose, the steadiness of their faith, and the depth of their gratitude.

THE END